WAKE UP
TO YOUR
DREAMS

WAKE UP
TO YOUR
DREAMS

Cover photography by:
Ray Boudreau

Digital Imaging by:
Jen Letch

SCHOLASTIC INC.
NEW YORK   TORONTO
LONDON   AUCKLAND   SYDNEY

ISBN 0-590-97908-6

Copyright © 1996 by Sandra Collier.
All rights reserved. Published by Scholastic Inc., 555 Broadway, New York, NY 10012, by arrangement with Scholastic Canada Ltd.

12 11 10 9 8 7 6 5 4 3 2 1   6 7 8 9/9 0 1/0

Printed in the U.S.A.   01

First Scholastic printing, September 1996

CONTENTS

WAKE UP
TO YOUR
DREAMS

# INTRODUCTION

When I was little, I had a recurring dream that was absolute torture for me. Just as I was falling asleep, a whirling blue object would show up in the corner of my room. It was like a spinning top, or a small flying saucer, and I knew it was going to get me. It gave off a weird bluish-green light that made me feel sick. I'd try to get out of bed but I'd be unable to move. I couldn't yell for help because my throat was paralyzed. The thing would come closer and closer, and the closer it came, the more I felt like I was going to throw up. Just when it was about an inch from my face, everything would go black.

Over time, I learned that when the spinning top appeared, nothing terrible was going to happen. I'd tell myself, It's okay, just relax, in a few minutes it will be over. But in the back of my mind I'd still be scared — maybe this time it really *was* going to get me.

But nighttime wasn't always terrifying. There were many other dreams that I loved having. Flying dreams were my favorite. Like this one:

I am flying through the air, making a kind of swimming movement with my arms — like I'm doing the breaststroke. It feels wonderful. Flying is just the best feeling in the whole world. I fly over my school, and some of my teachers look up and see me. They are totally amazed that I can fly.

In this dream, I felt free and happy — as if I could go anywhere and do anything. It was a great escape from rules and restrictions. And I wanted my teachers to see that I had magic powers — then maybe they would like me.

I've never lost my early fascination with dreams. Dreams have inspired and guided me throughout my whole life. In fact, this very book began with a dream I had many years ago. It "told" me to get a typewriter and start writing! For months, I hunted through antique shops and junk stores until I finally found the big old Underwood clunker that had appeared in my dream. Finding the typewriter was the easy part of fulfilling that dream — the writing part was a lot harder. Many times I stopped myself, thinking, This is crazy! It was only a dream! But whenever I wanted to give up, I'd have another dream that would seem to say, Don't give up, you're on the right track.

I have a tremendous love and respect for these mysterious phenomena we call dreams. Over the years I've listened to thousands of them, told to me by people from all over the world. Their messages have ranged from very basic and down-to-earth, like "stop smoking" or "eat more fruit," to the most profound spiritual revelations.

When you learn to understand your dreams, they will show you things you didn't know about yourself and other people. They will take you beneath the surface of things, and teach you to ask questions.

They can reveal secrets, as Josh, age 11, discovered:

> *I dreamed I came home from school and there was a Sold sign on our front lawn. I went inside, and there was another family living there. But our dog Sam was in the basement. He was crying. When I told my dream at breakfast, my mom and dad got these really strange looks, like their mouths sort of hung open. My mom said, "Who told you?" It turns out my dad got a new job, and we really were moving, but they didn't want to tell me till school was finished, because we wouldn't be able to take Sam with us!*

Dreams can help you make choices and encourage you to think for yourself, as Joy, 13, found:

> *One day at school, we were choosing our subjects for the next year, and I wanted to take French, but none of my friends were going to take it. I didn't know what to do, because I wanted to be with my friends, but I wanted to take French too. I dreamed that there was a whole bunch of people, and we were all in this big box. It was like a big*

room, and it was all gold, and nobody could get out. They were all panicking, but I kept really calm, and there was this button and I pushed it and a door opened and we got out. And then I was eating french fries! So I thought that my dream was helping me to take French, and that's what I did!

Sometimes dreams can protect you. Fred, age 10, dreamed:

I'm riding my bike and I start to go down this big hill. I'm going really fast, but when I try to slow down I don't have any brakes, and I just keep going faster and faster. The next day I checked my bike, and one of the brakes was worn right out!

And some dreams even tell the future. This is what happened to 14-year-old Dave:

I dreamed that my dad came home from work and he had coffee spilled all over his suit. At breakfast I told my dad my dream, and he said he wouldn't have any coffee at work, so the dream couldn't come true. All day my dad didn't have any coffee, but at the end of the day, my dad's boss came into the office and he was carrying a cup of coffee, and he tripped and spilled coffee all over my dad!

As you read further, you will learn more amazing facts about dreams. Chapter 1 will tell you how and why we dream. It also answers some of the most common questions people have about dreams.

4

Chapter 2 deals with specific dream themes, and Chapter 3 will give you practical information on understanding your own dreams.

Chapter 4, "Becoming a Master Dreamer," is for those of you who want to go even further and learn how you can use your dreams to solve problems, or have the kinds of dreams you want to have.

Read on, have fun and be amazed!

EVERYTHING YOU NEED TO KNOW ABOUT DREAMS

THE MAGIC KEY

I know my dream is trying to tell me something important, but I just can't understand it.
— Daria, age 12

Dreams can be mysterious — and sometimes baffling. The meaning seems to be locked away somewhere, beyond your understanding. But there is a key that can unlock any dream. It's called the Aha! feeling. It's as though a light gets turned on in your brain — suddenly you can see what was there all along. Some people feel a tingling inside, and some laugh or blush. Most describe it as something that just feels "right" in their bones.

The Aha! feeling is the most important tool you have to help you understand your dreams.

Ask Yourself!

People have come up with a lot of different ideas about dreams and what they mean. Some of them are pretty funny. For example, one book about dreams says, "If you dream of eating macaroni you will suffer reverses. A dream of cooking macaroni means that you will be the victim of fraud."

This book won't tell you what dreaming about macaroni means, but it will teach you ways to understand what your dreams mean to *you*. Sometimes, other people's suggestions and ideas can be useful and helpful. But the only person who can know for sure what your dreams mean is you.

When I first started listening to people's dreams, I sometimes jumped to conclusions. I would think I knew right away what a dream meant. But when I'd ask the dreamer, "What does a burning candle (or the moon, or the person in the dream) mean to you?" I would often discover that my first impression was wrong. Many times the dream would have a meaning to the dreamer that had never occurred to me.

Even today, I sometimes catch myself thinking, Oh yes, this dream means . . . When that happens, I stop myself and ask instead, I wonder what this dream might mean?

So I ask dreamers a lot of questions, as you will see. And it's by asking yourself these questions that you, too, will begin to find your answers.

> *I am going up the stairs in our house. I hear a creaking and I yell down to my mother and ask what it is. My mother says it's just the wind. I hear more creaking, and the door opens and at the bottom of the stairs I see this old lady. She's really, really old, and she's wearing a black cloak. She's carrying a basket of fruit, different kinds of fruit. She holds out a really shiny apple and asks, "Do you want a bite?" I've seen the movie Snow White so I say, "No," and then I wake up. But I've always been mad that I didn't say yes! I've always wondered what would have happened if I'd said yes!*
>
> — Samantha, age 12,
> recalling a dream she had when she was 7

THE MOST COMMON DREAM QUESTIONS

WHAT ARE DREAMS?

> *I knew I was dreaming but I didn't know it was called dreaming. I just thought I was doing something in my sleep.*
>
> — Stephen, age 7,
> recalling his early dreams at 2 and 3

Dreams are the thoughts and feelings you have while you are sleeping. You can have good dreams and bad dreams, just as you have good and bad feelings about yourself and your life.

Your dreams can be about the past, the present, or the future.

Art, age 11, dreamed about something that happened to him in the past:

> I was in a car accident a few years ago. For a long time afterwards I would dream about being in accidents, but in the dreams even worse things would happen.

Monique, age 8, dreamed about something in her present life:

> I heard on the news that hospitals were going to be shut down. It scared me because my dad works in a hospital. That night I dreamed his hospital closed down and my dad didn't have any work.

And Toby, 13, dreamed about the future:

> I was three when my mother was pregnant with my sister. I was really looking forward to the baby, and I'd dream that she had the baby. Only in the dream, it was always a boy!

WHERE DO DREAMS COME FROM?

Dreams come from you. They are the product of your brain's activity during a certain period of your sleep called REM sleep.

WHAT IS REM SLEEP?

REM is short for Rapid Eye Movement. This is a sleep state during which your eyes make quick, jerky movements — as though you were watching a fast game of ping-pong in your sleep. During REM sleep you breathe harder, your heart beats faster and you dream.

WHEN DO I HAVE REM SLEEP?

You have REM, or dream sleep, about every ninety minutes. When you sleep, your brain activity goes through different stages. If you could see your brainwaves traced out on paper, you would see a pattern that goes up and down like a row of stepladders.

DO I DREAM EVERY TIME I FALL ASLEEP?

If you imagine several stepladders standing in a row, you'll have some idea of what your sleep cycle looks like. Each ladder has four rungs going up, and four rungs going down. It looks like this:

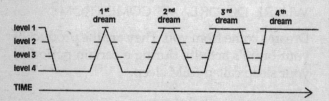

You begin your sleep at the top of the first ladder. This top rung is the lightest stage of sleep, and it has a fancy name: Level One NREM (non-REM) sleep. When you are up on the top rung, your brain is working much the same way as when you are awake. If someone were to wake you up during this stage of sleep, you'd probably say, "I wasn't asleep, I was thinking!"

Then you start to climb down the rungs of the sleep ladder. You descend to Level Two sleep, then Level Three and finally Level Four. Each rung takes you down into a deeper level of sleep. Level Four sleep is the deepest and most restful stage of sleep. You stay in Level Four for about half an hour, then you begin to climb the next ladder, through Level Three, Level Two and back to Level One again.

Now, after you have *returned* to Level One, you have your first dream of the night. This first dream is very short, usually just a few seconds long. Then it's back down the ladder again, to Level Four, and back up again.

Each trip down the ladder and back up again takes about ninety minutes. As the night progresses, you spend less time at the bottom level and more time at the top, in REM sleep. More time in REM sleep means longer dreams, so each dream you have during the night is longer than the one before. The last dream you have before waking is the longest — about an hour. This is the dream you're most likely to remember in the morning.

You go up and down the sleep ladder four to six times a night, so you have four to six dreams a night. That works out to about 40 dreams a week, or more than 2,000 dreams a year!

Your parents will probably only make it down the ladder to deep sleep once during the night. As people get older, they don't sleep as soundly.

DOES EVERYBODY DREAM?

I used to dream, but I don't anymore.
— Abby, age 14

Every person dreams every night. This has been proven many times in carefully controlled laboratory studies. People who say they never dream are mistaken. They do dream, but they forget their dreams upon awakening.

Blind people dream, even though they can't see. Those who were sighted at birth but lost their sight later on continue to dream pictures and colors, just like sighted people. People born blind dream sounds, actions, feelings and sensations — but not pictures or colors.

WHY DO WE DREAM?

We dream so that we can see what we are really like on the inside.
— Seth, age 14

. . . so we can play out our fantasies.
— Tracy, age 10

Your mind recalls things and mixes them up.
— Shakhar, age 13

Dreams are a way of working through what
happened that day.

— Jim, age 15

Dreams prepare you for life.

— Mina, age 12

Nobody really knows for sure why we
dream. Here are some of the most popular
theories:

Dreams are a kind of wish fulfillment. They
allow you to experience your innermost desires.
For example, Zeke, age 7, dreamed:

*I am perfect, and I never do anything wrong. I
have a math test — it's fifty pages and we only
have two minutes to do it. I get through it and I
get every question right.*

You might dream about getting presents, or
having lots of friends, or eating delicious foods.
Or you might dream about something bad
happening to your enemies. One 8-year-old girl
dreamed:

*There's a person I don't like at all. I dreamed she
died, and I was really happy.*

Dreams are a safety valve. They provide a
safe way to release feelings that can't be
expressed in waking life. Dreams let you express
angry feelings without actually hurting anyone.
A 10-year-old girl dreamed:

*Mr. T., one of my teachers — he's very sarcastic
and he makes me feel really stupid — is telling*

13

*me in front of the whole class that my workbook
is really messy. I pick up all my books and I
throw them at him, one at a time. I can't believe
I'm actually doing it! I would never really do
that, but when I woke up I felt good all day!*

Dreams protect sleep. For example, if a loud
noise starts to awaken you while you are
sleeping, you can dream about the noise and
keep on sleeping instead of waking up.

Mike, age 15, has experienced this more than
a few times! Mike loves his sleep, and he often
turns his wakeup call into a dream. One morning, after his mother called him to wake up for
school, Mike just kept on sleeping.

*I heard my mother calling me. She sounded like
she was really far away. I woke up, but I was
sitting at my desk at school. I'd been sleeping
with my head on my desk. So I said, "No sweat,
Mom, I'm already here!" I looked around, but
there was nobody else in the class, so I went back
to sleep! When I woke up [from this dream], I
was seriously late!*

Dreams mean nothing at all. When I was
at college, one of my professors told my class
that dreams are caused by random firings of the
neurons in the brain, and they have absolutely
no meaning. I disagree with this. I believe that a
dream that seems to mean nothing at all is only
a dream you don't yet understand.

Have you ever heard someone speaking in a
language you don't understand? At first, the

words don't make any sense to you. It sounds as though the person is talking nonsense. But if you pay attention and listen for awhile, you will start to recognize some of the sounds. They begin to have meaning.

In order to find meaning in your dreams, you have to learn the language. If you pay attention to your dreams and think about them, they *will* make sense to you. And understanding them benefits you.

WHAT HAPPENS IF WE DON'T DREAM?

Our minds would get all messed up and we wouldn't be able to think clearly.

— Jesse, age 10

Jesse is right. People who are prevented from dreaming have difficulty concentrating and suffer some memory loss. They feel tired, irritable, tense and anxious. When these people are able to start dreaming again, they actually dream *more*, as though they were trying to make up for their lost dreaming time!

Even scientists who believe that dreams mean nothing at all know that we *need* to dream. Dreaming plays an essential role in healthy brain functioning. Dreaming is important for our overall well-being, and the way we think and feel.

Dreaming is how the brain carries out its maintenance and repair. Your brain cannot rest itself while you are awake. When you sleep,

15

your brain goes "off-line" so it can process everything that you experienced while you were awake. The information in your brain is updated and organized. Anything that confused or upset you is analyzed.

DO BABIES DREAM?

Babies spend a lot of their time in REM sleep. Since kids and adults dream during REM sleep, it seems likely that babies are dreaming during REM sleep, too. Of course, they can't tell us one way or the other. However, I believe that babies do dream — most likely about the experiences and sensations they have encountered so far in their lives. Perhaps they dream about being fed or held. Sometimes babies grimace or frown in their sleep — maybe they're dreaming about something unpleasant, like feeling hungry or frightened. It's also possible that babies dream about the sensations they experienced in the womb before they were born.

DOES MY PET DREAM?

When my dog sleeps, he whines and yelps and twitches his legs like he's trying to run. It looks as if he is dreaming.

— Bruce, age 11

All mammals, and some birds, have REM sleep — so your pet probably does dream. But since animals can't talk, we can't know for sure.

DOES EVERYBODY DREAM IN COLOR?

Yes. Some people think they only dream in black and white, but if they were awakened in the middle of a dream they would remember colour. Sometimes part of a dream will be in black and white for a symbolic reason — maybe there is no "color," or variety, in the dreamer's life.

People are usually not aware of color unless it has some significance in the dream. Nigel, age 9, dreamed:

> *I'm in this place and all the people are wearing red baseball caps.*

Nigel has red hair, and he gets teased about it a lot. Although he acts like he doesn't care, he really wishes he didn't stand out so much. His dream expresses his wish to blend in and not feel different.

WHY ARE DREAMS SO HARD TO REMEMBER?

> *Dreams depart so quickly.*
> — Lorie, age 13

There are two kinds of memory: long-term and short-term. When you look up a number in the telephone book you will probably remember it just long enough to dial the number, and then forget it. That's short-term memory. If you want to remember the number, you have to memorize it — or write it down! Most dreams are like

17

telephone numbers. Unless you do something special to help you remember them later, they will be quickly forgotten.

A very vivid, shocking or intense dream is easier to remember because it makes a deeper impression on you. An amazing dream like flying or scoring the winning goal for your team will be more easily remembered. So will dreams that upset you. Sometimes you can't forget a bad dream even if you want to!

If you are awakened in the middle of a dream, you will have no trouble recalling it. If you are awakened five minutes *after* a dream, you will probably only remember parts of it. If you wake up more than *ten* minutes after a dream, you will most likely have forgotten most or all of it. Usually the dream you remember best is the last dream of your sleep — the one you have just before you wake up.

WHAT ARE NIGHTMARES?

Nightmares and night terrors are often lumped together as the same thing, but they are in fact very different.

A nightmare is an extremely frightening and upsetting dream. It is much more unpleasant than an ordinary bad dream. Usually the dreamer feels threatened in some way:

Me and all my family are in the kitchen, but my dad looks really strange. He looks like a bad guy. These men storm in, a gang with guns. They

18

*shoot at my dad and kill him. All the others run
away. I try to hide, but this bad guy keeps
chasing me. I run outside and yell to our
neighbors to help me, but they don't hear me,
and they can't see me. It's like I'm a ghost. I run
up and down, and nobody helps me.*

— Laura, age 11

Because a nightmare is so frightening, it
usually makes a vivid impression. You're very
likely to remember it in the morning.

*I am in the woods, cutting down trees with a
chainsaw, and the chainsaw jumps on my arms
and cuts off both my arms. My dad and my
brother and my stepmother are there and they are
all laughing.*

— Chris, age 12

Nightmares can be triggered by upsetting
events in your life, like changing schools,
moving, violence, divorce or illness. Megan has
to have daily injections of insulin because she
has diabetes. She says:

*I have nightmares that a purple monster tries to
take my needle away. Another time I dreamed a
policeman gave me a needle and I was going to
die.*

— Megan, age 5

Nightmares can also be caused by disturbing
TV programs, films and books. You might not
think a TV show or video has upset you, but if
you have nightmares afterwards then you can
be sure it has. And you don't even have to see
something disturbing — even hearing about

19

something upsetting or gruesome can affect your dreams.

Once I watched Nightmare on Elm Street. *I had bad dreams for a long time afterwards. I sometimes still have bad dreams about Freddy. The other night I dreamed that a guy was in the house, and he got rough — he threatened me with a coat hanger — so we were struggling. The door got busted down, and Freddy Krueger was standing there. He said, "I'm here," and started walking over. I went for the back door. Freddy slashed the guy, and then came after me.*

— Mel, age 15

Everyone has nightmares from time to time. Having a nightmare once in a while is nothing to worry about. However, if you are bothered by frequent nightmares there might be something in your life that is upsetting you. It would be helpful for you to talk to someone about it.

My little brother sometimes wakes up screaming and crying. He's really terrified. It takes about half an hour for him to settle down, but in the morning he doesn't remember a thing!

— Sirhan, age 16

A night terror is different from a nightmare. It is a sleep disorder that occurs during Level Four sleep, the deepest stage of sleep. There's no story to a night terror — it's a sensation of acute panic. The sleeper awakens suddenly and violently. Some people actually throw themselves right out of bed! Often the sleeper will wake up screaming. If you have younger brothers or sisters, you have probably seen or heard them awaken from a night terror, terrified, crying and unable to say much, except perhaps that something was after them.

People who suffer from night terrors experience all or most of the following:

- ❖ sudden or violent awakening
- ❖ screaming or crying out upon awakening
- ❖ feeling of extreme terror
- ❖ racing heartbeat
- ❖ body wet with perspiration
- ❖ rapid, shallow breathing, sometimes gasping for air
- ❖ attacks occurring during first half of the night
- ❖ no memory of attack in the morning

Occasional night terrors are upsetting, but they do not usually mean anything is wrong. They do pass away with time, as the nervous system matures. However, if you are having night terrors very often you should tell your parents or your family doctor.

IS SLEEPWALKING RELATED TO DREAMING?

Sleepwalking is a very different state from dreaming. It is caused by a disturbance in the sleep cycle, and occurs during Level Two sleep. Scott's mother describes his experience:

Scott started sleepwalking when he was six years old. He would get out of bed — fast asleep — and walk into the kitchen. He'd go straight to the fridge and open the door. He didn't take any food out or anything. He'd just stand there, staring into the fridge. His eyes were wide open, but he was sound asleep. It was just the strangest thing to see! He'd stare into the fridge for maybe a minute or two, and then he'd close the door and walk back to his bedroom and get back into bed. In the morning he wouldn't remember a thing. This went on for several months. Maybe I should mention that Scott started sleepwalking after his baby sister was born.

Sleepwalking is very common in children. Nearly half of all children walk in their sleep. It happens most often in kids between the ages of 11 and 12.

Most people stop sleepwalking by the time they reach their teens. However, some adults continue to sleepwalk. A few have even gone outdoors and started their cars while they were sound asleep!

The tendency to sleepwalk is inherited. It can be triggered by sleep deprivation, fever, certain medications or stress. (For Scott, stress about his baby sister was almost certainly a factor.)

When sleepwalkers are awakened they are surprised to find themselves up. They don't have any memory of a dream.

If you discover someone in your family sleepwalking, it is best to lead him gently back to bed. Try to avoid waking him suddenly, because this will be frightening and confusing for him. If you must wake him up, try to do it gently.

There is still a lot we don't understand about sleepwalking. But there is nothing wrong with you if you sleepwalk. You will most likely outgrow it before long.

DO KIDS DREAM DIFFERENTLY FROM ADULTS?

Kids have many more nightmares than adults.

We go to a movie and there's a witch on the screen. And then she jumps off the screen and comes after me.

— Sally, age 5

Kids dream a lot more about animals.

I dreamed about a talking lamb. It was my friend. It protected me. I just loved it.

— Cassie, age 7

I dreamed my rabbit was eating cereal for breakfast.

— Barry, age 5

Children dream more about bad things happening to them. They also have more dreams about being chased and attacked than adults do.

There's a Tyrannosaurus Rex after me. It's going to eat me up.

— Bela, age 6

I'm in the jungle with my dad. There's a giant spider after us.

— Wally, age 8

Usually the dreams of young children are less complicated and easier to understand than those of adults.

I'm throwing all my toys and books all over the room and Mommy comes in and gets mad and yells at me and I laugh at her and throw more things around and Mommy gets madder and then she falls through a hole in the floor.

— Stacey, age 3

They are also straightforward. For example, when the fire marshal came to her nursery school, 4-year-old Brenda dreamed:

There is a fire. The firemen come to put it out.

Very young children often dream about sleeping and eating.

I dreamed I was sleeping in the bathtub. I was happy.

— William, age 3

When I was little, I dreamed about food a lot. Eggs, sausages, hamburgers and ice cream!

— Clara, age 7

WHAT ARE RECURRING DREAMS?

Recurring dreams are dreams that you have again and again. They are very common. Most people have them at some point in their lives.

Recurring dreams usually represent unresolved issues in the dreamer's life.

> *When I was little I always wore dresses, and when I got dressed I'd forget to put underwear on. So I had this dream over and over again that I was going to school in a dress and I didn't have any underwear on and I'd have to be really careful.*
>
> — Ghislaine, age 11

Once the problem has been resolved, the recurring dream always stops. You can imagine what a good feeling that is!

Sometimes people have pleasant recurring dreams:

> *I have a recurring dream that I am swimming in the water with dolphins. It's my favorite dream. I love having it.*
>
> — Jyll, age 9

If you have pleasant recurring dreams, you might want to pay attention to *when* you are having them. If they come when you are upset or having problems, it is likely that your dreams are trying to help you through a difficult time by reminding you that there are good feelings and good times in life too. We will explore recurring dreams further in Chapter 3.

WHAT ARE DAYDREAMS?

> *I like to daydream that I am a kung fu master. These guys in gangs come after me and I beat them all up.*
>
> — Charles, age 9

Daydreams are very different from night dreams. The most obvious difference is that when you daydream you are awake, and your brain is functioning differently than when you are asleep.

A daydream is a fantasy. It is something you wilfully imagine and can control completely. You can start and stop it whenever you wish. You can change the storyline however you like.

A daydream is not as intense or exciting as a night dream. This is because your brain responds to a dream experience the same way it does to waking events. If you dream that you are running an Olympic race, your brain actually orders your muscles to move, just as though you were really running.

But, of course, you don't *actually* move while you dream. Your body produces special chemicals during REM sleep which cause a temporary paralysis of your large muscles. If you weren't restrained this way, you would throw yourself out of bed whenever you dreamed you were moving!

A night dream can feel absolutely real in every way, even though you might be doing something fantastic, like turning into an animal or swimming to the bottom of the sea.

There are no surprises in daydreams, because in a daydream you think about what you *want* to think about. A night dream will bring you images or experiences that are new or surprising to you.

A good way to understand the difference between a daydream and a night dream is to think of your closet. A daydream is like the things you have at the front of your closet — the things you use every day.

But a night dream is more like the back of your closet, where things are often forgotten. The back of your closet might be where you keep things that are broken or that you want to save. Perhaps there are things you want to hide there as well. It's darker at the back of the closet than at the front. It's usually messier back there too.

You daydream about things that are "up front" and close to you. Daydreams are in the light. You know about them. But night dreams happen in the dark, where things are more difficult to see. You might not be as familiar with these things, but they can be very important.

DOES WHAT I ATE FOR DINNER AFFECT MY DREAMS?

> *I had chili for dinner. Is that why I dreamed the house was on fire?*
>
> —Derek, age 13

Sometimes what you eat can upset your stomach. Indigestion can disturb your sleep and cause an upsetting dream. But an outside influence like what you eat cannot fully explain a dream.

Sometimes when a child is very young, a full bladder may begin to wake her up. But instead of waking, she may dream that she is already in the bathroom and that it is okay to let go. In the morning, everybody discovers the bed is wet, and sometimes the child is made to feel guilty. But the accident was really caused by the dream!

Sometimes when I hear things it goes into my dream. My sister was calling me, but I dreamed it was my gym teacher speaking to me.
— Vicky, age 9

You feel and hear many things while you sleep. You feel your sheets and blankets on your skin, the warmth or coolness of your room. You hear sounds from outside, like rain, sirens or animal sounds. Only a very few of these sounds and sensations become a part of your dreams. And when outside influences *do* get into your dreams, your state of mind influences the end result.

For example, Bob and Carol both had dreams during a loud thunderstorm. Bob dreamed he was at a picnic and firecrackers went off, while Carol dreamed she was in the subway and a bomb exploded.

Remember the dream Mike had when his mother tried to wake him up? That is another example of an outside influence affecting a dream.

IF I DIE IN A DREAM, WILL I HAVE A HEART ATTACK FROM THE SHOCK?

Absolutely not. Many people have dreamed of their own deaths and nothing terrible happened to them. Usually what occurs is that the dream continues and the "dead" dreamer continues to be in the dream, but perhaps in some changed way. Joe, age 13, "died" in one of his dreams:

I see my funeral, and a little flash of my grave.
I'm up in heaven. I feel happy.

Remember, all kinds of things are possible in dreams. You can fly, you can see around corners, you can change into an animal — and you can die in a dream and still be perfectly alive.

Another common misbelief is that if you dream you are falling and you actually hit the ground in the dream, you will die. I believed this myself when I was growing up. Every time I had a falling dream I would try to wake myself up before I hit bottom. Sometimes I would wake up with a terrible jolt when I was just a few inches from the ground. It was really an awful experience.

But then one day I read in a magazine that the best thing to do during a falling dream is to actually let yourself fall and find out where you'd land. So every night, before I went to sleep, I told myself that if I had another falling dream I would let myself fall.

Then one night it happened. I dreamed I was falling and I kept falling until I finally hit the bottom. And do you know what? It didn't hurt at all. It was like landing on a big soft cushion. It was a very nice feeling, quite different from the one I had feared.

And best of all is this: I've never had a falling dream since!

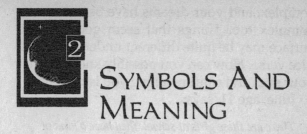

Symbols And Meaning

The Dream Message

*It's the first day of camp. My mom is going to get
an apple for my lunch but it grows legs and runs
away, and it's the only apple in the house. So
then we get a banana, but it turns into a
telephone. Then we get two kiwis but they turn
into two tennis balls. We catch the apple and cut
off its legs and put it into my lunch.*

— Rebecca, age 9

What in the world does this dream mean? If you
were to take it at face value, it wouldn't make
any sense at all. So why don't dreams just say
what they mean? If a dream contains a message,
why doesn't it just come right out and tell us?

Well, very often dreams do say things very
clearly.

*Sometimes I dream we are living in our old house
and we're all together and we're happy again, the
way we used to be.*

— Ray, age 15

When you were little, your dreams were
easier to understand. But now your life is more

31

complex, and your dreams have become more complex too. Things that seem good on the surface may be quite different underneath, and vice versa. How can you possibly know if what your eyes and ears are telling you is the truth?

Julie, age 11, says:

There are these girls at school, they have a kind of club. They never paid any attention to me, but one day they started being really nice to me. They asked me to eat lunch with them and stuff. And then one of the girls, she wanted to borrow some money from me. I lent it to her, but she couldn't pay me back. And then she wanted to borrow some more money, and that night I dreamed that we were all having lunch, and she gave me this apple. It was like this really big, red apple. It just looked so delicious, but when I bit into it, it was all full of worms.

This dream helped Julie to see that what looked good on the surface was really rotten underneath. She decided not to lend the girl any more money. And sure enough, the girls stopped being friendly to Julie. This showed Julie that their friendship was not genuine.

Dreams teach you one of the most important and difficult lessons to learn: there is more going on in your life than appears on the surface. And one of the best ways dreams show you this is by using symbols.

A symbol is something that represents something else. When you call someone a rat, you mean that person is false and untrustworthy.

When you call someone a chicken, you really mean he is afraid. The words rat and chicken are used to stand for something else. They are symbols.

One of the reasons dreams can be difficult to understand at first is that so much of dream language is symbolic.

How Dreams Use Symbols

Dreams use symbols to show you things that are invisible, like feelings. How would you express love in a dream? What about a quality, like goodness? You would not be able to describe them directly. You would have to use something else to represent them.

Fear will be represented in a dream by something frightening, like a monster or a kidnapper. An important value like honesty might appear as a precious jewel.

> *There was this lady. She was a friend of my mother's. She's dead now, but when she was alive she was sick a lot and she complained about everything. When I'm depressed, she shows up in my dreams.*
>
> — Claire, age 9

This person is a symbol of depression for Claire.

More than one feeling or thought can be symbolized in a dream.

> *After my grandpa died I dreamed that he came into my room and sat on my bed. He gave me his*

gold watch that he wore on a chain, and said,
"This is for you." When I thought about the
dream, it seemed to me that the watch was his
love. But now I think it's more than that. It's like
it's also everything he taught me.

— Pat, age 14

Sometimes the different feelings you have in a dream are conflicting ones. You could probably think of many things that you have mixed feelings about. School might mean good and bad things to you at the same time. And think back to a time when you did something brave, like jumping off a diving board. You very likely felt excited and afraid all at once.

It is normal to have conflicting feelings about important things in your life. Most of us do. You want to be free, but you need security too. You want to be good, but sometimes you are tempted to be bad. Your dreams show you the conflicts in your feelings.

When I was 4 years old I dreamed about a neighborhood boy named Jimmy:

I'm jumping up and down on Jimmy D.'s
stomach. I'm really stomping on him. But all of a
sudden Jimmy's stomach splits open and his guts
spill out. I get really scared. I think I have killed
him. And then I wake up.

At the time, I didn't tell anybody about this dream, because I was afraid it meant I was a bad person. But many years later I understood that the dream was about my own conflicting feelings of anger, fear and helplessness.

Jimmy was much older than me — one of the "big boys" — and he made my life miserable. He would hide behind bushes and jump out at me. He threw stones at me, broke my toys and teased me. I was helpless in waking life, so I took my anger out in my dream. But I was also afraid of my anger. I had once seen one of my cousins being beaten up. I remembered how he had been covered in blood. To my young mind, he had been "split open." My angry feelings frightened me — and the dream expressed this conflict.

It can be difficult to accept your own negative feelings. You might dream that someone else is doing wrong, not you.

I dreamed that my dolls came to life and they killed my brother.

— Margaret, age 7

In this dream, the dolls expressed Margaret's angry feelings so she didn't have to.

DREAM DICTIONARIES

Have you ever seen a dream dictionary? This kind of book lists many different dream symbols. You can look up your dream in it and it will tell you the meaning. Some of these "meanings" are pretty funny. Here's an example:

To dream of drinking from a jug predicts that you will be lucky in the next lottery.

Of course, different dream dictionaries say different things.

Let's suppose you had a dream that you were having a haircut. One dream dictionary says:

Because hair comes from the head it stands for thoughts: the different types of hair represent different kinds of thoughts.

Another says:

Hair is a symbol of attractiveness in women, and strength in men.

And a third says:

It is a fortunate omen to dream of finding a hair when cutting butter.

Which one of them is right? How can you tell? The only reliable guide is your instinct — the Aha! feeling.

Karen, age 12, had a dream about her hair — let's see what she thinks:

KAREN: *I dreamed I got my hair cut. I didn't like it.*

QUESTION: *Tell me about your hair.*

K: *I don't look good in short hair. One time my big sister took me to get my hair cut. I didn't want this guy to cut my hair, but my sister told me I would like it. Well, it was really gross. He cut my hair off really, really short — above my ears. I was crying. I hated it, I just hated it.*

Q: *How did you feel in the dream when you were getting your hair cut?*

K: *Awful! Like, Oh no, I don't want this to happen.*

Q: *Is that happening now? Something you don't want to happen?*

K: *Yes! My sister! She wants me to switch bedrooms with her. She wants me to have her room and she'll take mine, but I don't want to. I like my room.*

Q: *What could you do now that you didn't do before, when the guy cut your hair?*

K: *Say no! But if I do, she'll get mad at me.*

Q: *How did you feel when you got the haircut you didn't want?*

K: *Awful! I wish I'd said no. If I remember how bad I felt, then I don't care if my sister gets mad at me. It's my hair, and my room!*

Q: *What would you say hair means to you?*

K: *Well, it's how I look. But it's more than that. It means having control over something that's mine.*

Each person's dream symbols are unique and personal. When 10-year-old Jo Anne dreams about cats, for example, they symbolize scary things that hurt her. Jo Anne doesn't like cats. Her grandmother had a cat that would bite and scratch Jo Anne when she went to visit. Jo Anne was afraid of the cat, and her grandmother's house was dark and frightening. Jo Anne is also allergic to cats — they make her break out in hives.

But when Melissa, age 9, dreams about cats, they represent good feelings, like warmth and softness and comfort. Cats also bring back Melissa's special memory of going to the

Humane Society with her father to pick out a kitten for her birthday.

So you can see how the same symbol can mean very different things to different people.

THE TOP TEN DREAM THEMES

Although dream images depend on the person dreaming them, some common dream themes seem to have almost universal meanings. Here are the most common ones.

As you read this section, please remember that it is a general guide only — these are not the *only* meanings. Only *you* can decide if these explanations apply to your dreams.

1. DREAMS OF BEING CHASED

Young people often dream about being chased. A big reason for this is that when you're young, people always seem to be after you to do things. You are constantly being reminded to sit up straight, do your homework, be polite, and so on.

> *I get chased a lot in my dreams. In one dream I had I'm playing at the beach. I'm in the water and a giant killer whale comes for me. I try to run up the beach but it's too hard to run on the sand and I keep slipping back. I keep running but I keep slipping back, and the whale keeps grabbing me. I just keep trying to stumble up the beach.*
> —Jan, age 12

Being chased can also mean that you feel threatened by something or someone in your life.

A guy has a car, and the car opens up and shoots lasers. It shoots at the guy who lives across the street and he dies. Then the car comes over to our house and chases me. It shoots me but I don't die. We go into our old house and I'm covering my neck. There is blood on it.

— Nena, age 9

A chasing dream might uncover a problem that you are trying not to face. Until you address it, the problem won't go away.

When you have a dream about being chased, ask yourself these questions:

 ✧ Is there something or someone I'm trying to get away from?
 ✧ Do I feel guilty about something? Am I afraid of being caught?
 ✧ What's going on in my life that I don't want to face?
 ✧ Am I pushing myself too hard? Is somebody else?

The best way to stop being chased in your dreams is to just stop running. Tell yourself that you will turn and face whoever or whatever is chasing you. You can learn more about how to take control of your dreams in Chapter 4.

Quite often in a chasing dream you will feel stuck, held back or physically weak. Ian, age 12, had this dream:

Someone is after me. I try to run away, but my legs are like lead. They weigh a ton. I try and try, but I can hardly lift them. I can hardly move at all.

If you have this kind of dream, you probably hate it. Most people do! You are trying, trying, trying with all your might to do something or get away from someone and you just can't. You feel stuck. No matter how hard you try, you're just not getting anywhere.

I'm trying to run, but the wind is blowing against me. It's so strong I can't get anywhere. There's a man behind me. He's going to kidnap me.
— Penny, age 11

When you have this kind of dream, ask yourself:

✧ What do I feel helpless or frustrated about?
✧ Who or what is holding me back?
✧ Is there something in *me* that is holding me back?

A similar dream frustration is being unable to talk. You want to call for help but no words come out of your mouth.

In my dream someone is after me. He's a kidnapper. I'm trying to shout out for help, but I can't.
— Isaac, age 10

If you are unable to speak in a dream, ask:

◇ What is it that feels impossible for me to say?

My mom expects me to babysit for my little brother. I want to be with my friends. I can't tell my mom — she works so hard.

— Drew, age 15

When Drew did speak to his mother they were able to work out a schedule, so now Drew has more time to spend with his friends.

2. DREAMS OF LOSS, ABANDONMENT OR KIDNAPPING

Robbers break into our house. They want to take me away. I have to hold on to my mother's and my father's arms so they won't take me away. I have to hold on with all my might.

— Chris, age 6

Everyone worries about losing the people they love. When you have dreams about loss, you might want to think about what has happened to trigger these fears.

When you don't feel safe, you may dream about kidnappers or being kidnapped. You might worry about your safety after hearing or reading something frightening.

I am a tourist somewhere. A bomb goes off — a big one — in the town square. Everyone is really scared. I am helping the people who are hurt. The terrorists come back and kidnap me.

— Lana, age 14

You might also worry about being abandoned. Anna, age 14, had this dream when she found out her mother was ill with cancer:

Somehow I'm a tiny baby, about an inch long, nearly invisible. I'm in an antique store. I put myself in the drawer of a desk and wait for my brothers. But they leave without me. I wait for a long time. Then I come out. I ask the little old lady in charge if I can call my mother. She looks for the telephone. It's a strange telephone with a plant growing on it. I call my mother. "Come get me, you forgot me, I've been here all the time."

If one of your parents has died, or if your parents have separated, you might worry that your mother or father will meet somebody new and stop loving you.

I dreamed me and my brother were lost in the woods, just like in "Hansel and Gretel," but the witch turned out to be my mom. This was the scariest dream I've ever had.

— Luc, age 8

If you dream about being kidnapped or abandoned, try asking yourself:

✦ What doesn't feel safe to me?
✦ What would help me to feel more safe?
✦ Who can I talk to about my worries?

3. A DEAD PERSON SHOWS UP IN A DREAM

I dreamed my grandpa came back to life. It scared

*my parents — they thought he was a zombie, but
he wasn't to me.*

— Andre, age 7

It is very common to dream about people who
have died, especially if you had strong feelings
about them when they were alive. Perhaps you
miss the person and the good times you had
together.

*I dreamed my Nana was alive and we went over
to her house and she gave us presents.*

— Nancy, age 10

Although the person is dead, what he or
she stood for is still alive in you. You can
continue to uphold the values and virtues
you learned from that person.

If it was someone you loved, the dream is a
way of being with that person again.

*My grandpa died last year. I didn't get to see him
very much, because he lived so far away. I
wanted to know him more, and he showed up in
my dream. I actually didn't know how much I
loved him until he died. I can't believe how much
I miss him.*

— Kally, age 8

If you dream about a dead person, ask
yourself:

✧ What good things did this person bring
to me?

✧ How does being with this person again
help me?

43

If the person was someone you didn't like, something in your life is making you feel the way that person made you feel.

⋄ How did this person make me feel when he or she was alive?
⋄ What is making me feel unhappy?

If you dream about death you may worry that you or someone close to you is going to die. But most dreams about death are not really about someone dying.

In order to understand a death dream, ask yourself:

⋄ What *feels* dead to me right now?
⋄ What in my life is coming to an end?

A death dream may show you that a friendship is over or that you are no longer interested in a sport or hobby. But remember, the dream only indicates how you feel right now. For example, if you think your dream means a friendship has died, maybe there's something you can do to bring it back to life. In dreams, death does not have to mean *forever*, the way it does in real life.

You might dream about the death of someone you don't like or who makes you angry. You may even dream that *you* die:

I hate myself in the dream and I jump into a swamp and I die. I'm glad to die.

44

The 5-year-old girl who had this dream had gotten into trouble at home. Parents and teachers can sometimes forget how very bad kids can feel about things.

- ✧ Is there someone I wish would go away? If so, why? What would change for me?
- ✧ Is there another way I could solve my problem?

If there has been a death in your family recently, you may have dreams about grieving:

My grandpa died a few weeks ago. I dreamed that we were in a big room, like a gym, but there was nothing in it, only a long empty table. My whole family was there. We were huddled together like we were really poor and cold and we were all crying on account of my grandpa dying. The whole dream was of us crying and it was really, really real. You know when you cry really hard? It was like that. When I woke up, I felt relieved. Like when you really cry a lot and then you feel relieved? Like that. I think the dream was about letting go of my grandpa.

— Kara, age 11

Sometimes a dream about death helps to prepare you when you know someone who is very sick and soon going to die. Shortly before 16-year-old Kerry's brother died of leukemia, Kerry dreamed:

Donny goes into the bathroom sick. I see Donny as he used to be, before he got sick. I'm scared, and then I see Donny as he used to be go into Donny's body like it is today. I start screaming, "Don't do it," but his healthy body goes into his sick body. Donny comes out of the bathroom and says, "This is it." And he lies down on the floor and dies.

4. FLYING DREAMS

I'm flying over Dragon Mountain and the sun is setting. I don't really pay attention to how I'm flying. I don't go, Oh, I'm flying! I'm paying more attention that I can fly and see how beautiful everything is, the tops of the trees . . . and that I can do whatever I want. When I fly it's like floating or dancing.

— Kirsten, age 12

In dreams, people fly in many different ways.

Flying dreams are the best! I can go wherever I want. When I fly it's like I'm walking on thin air. I go as high as I want.

— Raj, age 13

Some people fly with their arms outstretched, like Superman. Others make a kind of swimming motion. Still others let someone or something else do the flying:

In my flying dreams I'm in something that is flying. One time I was in the house in The Wizard of Oz. Sometimes I'm in a bird's stomach and it's flying.

— Mimi, age 8

Flying in dreams can show that you're feeling high — on top of the world. Flying often means letting go, unleashing your imagination, creativity or spirituality. It can express a need to be free and spontaneous.

Some people love their flying dreams, others are frightened by them. People who are frightened by their flying dreams may be afraid of their imaginations, or they may have been told not to aim too high in life. When flying is difficult in dreams, it sometimes means the dreamer has a problem he or she is trying to "rise above."

When you have a flying dream, ask yourself:

◇ Is there something I'm trying to overcome?
◇ Am I using imagination or fantasy to escape from a problem ?
◇ Do I need more fun, more lightness in my life?
◇ Are there people I "look down on"?

5. DREAMS OF BEING NAKED, OR WEARING UNDERWEAR OR PAJAMAS IN PUBLIC

I'm walking down the street and all of a sudden I look down and I realize I'm not wearing any clothes, so I run home, but when I get home I can't find anything to wear. I keep looking and looking, but I can't find anything to wear.
— Fran, age 10

Being naked in a dream can represent a feeling of being exposed or vulnerable.

I dreamed I left my clothes at school. I went home in my underwear. People were laughing at me. I was embarrassed.

— Hal, age 9

How you feel in the dream is very important. Many people feel absolutely mortified when they first begin having naked dreams. But over time, as they gain more confidence in themselves, they stop feeling embarrassed. They realize they can be themselves in front of other people without feeling ashamed.

If you dream that you are wearing your pajamas or underwear while everyone else is dressed in daytime clothes, think back to the previous day. Ask yourself:

✦ Did I feel out of place?
✦ Did I behave in some way that set me apart?
✦ Did I reveal something that I feel insecure about?

Again, it is your feeling about being in your pajamas or your underwear that determines the meaning of the dream.

Another thing to think about is how other people react to you in the dream. Are they comfortable with you, or are they laughing and pointing?

*When I'd dream that I didn't have any clothes
on, I used to feel, like, total shame. I'd be going,
Oh no, this can't be happening! But now it's not
a big deal. I think that's because I feel pretty good
about myself now. I'm not so influenced by what
other people think.*

— Lee, age 17

6. BATHROOM DREAMS

*I'm in a huge public restroom. There are rows
and rows of toilets. Hundreds of them. But they
are all plugged and overflowing, not working,
out of order. The place really stinks. It is so gross!
All these toilets, but not one I can use.*

— Jack, age 14

Going to the bathroom is one of the most common things people dream about. Bathroom dreams are about things that make you feel embarrassed — things you might not want anyone else to know about. They might not necessarily be bad things — usually they aren't at all. But for some reason, you feel that they are bad and try to keep them hidden. That's when you'll have a dream that you are in a public bathroom, and there is no door to the cubicle, and everyone can see you. Or that someone walks in on you while you are sitting on the toilet!

*I'm in a public restroom. It doesn't look like
anyone is in it, but all the doors are locked.
Finally I find one that's open, but its toilet is
upside down!*

— Anna, age 9

Maybe the toilet is all plugged up and overflowing. The bathroom might be horribly dirty and smelly. It is normal and natural to have such dreams. All it means is that you feel sensitive or ashamed about something that you believe should be kept hidden or private.

Dreams about plugged-up toilets often mean that the dreamer has no outlet for unpleasant thoughts or feelings. When this happens it's important to talk to someone you trust. This is always better than staying "plugged up."

Sometimes a bathroom dream comes when you've done something you really should feel ashamed about. Don't be afraid to be honest with yourself. If you don't feel good about what you have done, perhaps you can correct it.

The bathroom is the place where you wash and get clean. You might dream about washing yourself or being in dirty water when there's something weighing on your conscience.

If you have a bathroom dream, ask yourself these questions:

❖ Have I done or said something I feel ashamed or embarrassed about?
❖ Is there something I want to "come clean" about?

7. WATER DREAMS

I dream about being in water a lot. Usually I'm swimming in a lake. The water is warm and clear, and I find all these dolphins. We swim

together, the dolphins and me. It's just so
wonderful.

— Lori, age 13

Bodies of water show up very often in dreams. The first thing for you to do is identify the nature of the water. If it is clear and supportive, then it could represent life and creativity. The ocean is the source of all life. You began your life in water, in the womb.

If the water is dangerous and threatening, it might indicate that you are feeling unsafe.

I'm in this river. The water is black — it's really gross and disgusting. I'm trying to swim across to the other side, but there is all this stuff in the water, like garbage and big pieces of wood, branches and stuff. I keep bumping into things. It's dark and I can't see. There are jellyfish in the water that sting me.

Kyle, age 16, had this dream many times while he was living in a foster home he hated. Some questions to ask yourself are:

✧ How do I feel in the water? Comfortable? Frightened? Strong?
✧ What is the experience like? Pleasurable? Frightening? Challenging?

Dreams about drowning could reflect a concern about water safety. After Eric had a frightening experience in the water, he had several dreams about drowning. Then he signed up for a course in water safety and his drowning

51

dreams stopped. If you dream about water and danger, ask yourself:

- ✧ Have I recently been in a situation where water safety rules were being broken?
- ✧ Is boating or diving equipment I use unsafe?

If you are afraid of water, you might want to consider taking swimming lessons or a course in lifesaving.

Or maybe you're feeling overwhelmed by something in your life. When 13-year-old Ali's parents got a divorce, he started to do poorly at school. He had trouble concentrating and fell behind in his work.

I started having dreams that I was drowning. There isn't much story to the dream. Usually I'm swimming around — it's a good dream at first — but then it gets all cloudy and the waves get big and go over my face, and then I realize I've gone under three times, and that I'm drowning.

Ali felt that he couldn't keep on top of his work. He was worried about his parents. He felt as if he was "going under." Usually, having a dream about drowning means you need help with a problem.

Dreams of tidal waves come at times when you're feeling overwhelmed by something out of your control, say, a family problem or illness. They can also appear when you fall in love and are overwhelmed by feelings you've never felt before.

If you dream of a tidal wave, ask yourself:

✧ Do you feel overwhelmed by something that is happening to you?
✧ Who can you go to for help?

Dreams about frozen water, like snow or ice, might point to some kind of emotional coldness in the dreamer's life. Heather, age 15, had a crush on J., a boy in her class. Although he was never nice to Heather, she kept on calling him at home and buying him snacks at school. One night she dreamed:

I'm driving my father's car. I see J. and stop to give him a ride. He gets in, but as soon as he does, the car fills up with snow. He also seems to have a big icicle in his mouth.

This dream helped Heather to see she was wasting her time on J.!

You might find it helpful to ask:

✧ Who or what feels "cold" to me?
✧ Am I frozen with fear about something?

8. FALLING DREAMS

Many people dream about falling when they are afraid of failure, or of disappointing someone. For example, 9-year-old Steven had several falling dreams after he failed math at school:

*I'm Rollerblading with my sister, and I fall on
the ground. My sister keeps going.*

Steven felt that he had disappointed his
parents — that he had fallen out of favor with
them. He worried that they preferred his sister
because she was a better student.

Falling dreams can also be about insecurity,
as 12-year-old Pat's dream illustrates:

*I dreamed I was on top of the mountain K2. My
dad fell down into a big crevasse. I was scared.*

And Rosa, age 11, says:

*When I didn't know how to swim, I dreamed
about falling into the pool and hitting my head.*

Some questions you can ask are:

◇ Have I fallen out of favor with
  someone?
◇ Do I feel worried or insecure about
  something?
◇ What would help me feel safer?

Now and then a falling dream may be a signal
that you need to come back to earth. Perhaps you
have been "flying away" — daydreaming too
much.

Sometimes it can be pleasant to fall. Dreams
can help you learn that a fall or failure is not the
end of the world. Maybe you need to overcome
your own fear of falling — to remember that you

fell plenty of times when you were little and were able to pick yourself up and keep going. Don't be afraid to fall. Falling is part of life!

9. LOSING IMPORTANT THINGS

Your teeth and hair are important to your appearance, so dreams about losing hair or teeth often come when you are worried about how you look.

> *I'm with my friends at the beach. I look in a mirror and see my front tooth is broken off. Then some big chips and layers of other teeth fall off. I hold them in my hand. They're like pieces of fingernails. I drop the pieces on the ground. My friends want to move to another part of the beach. We go, but it's more crowded there. I am very worried about my teeth, and look again in a mirror.*
>
> — Jeff, age 14

Jeff had this dream after finding out that he hadn't made the basketball team. He was worried about how his friends would see him, how he would look in their eyes. He felt he had "lost face" with them. He was also concerned that girls would see him as unattractive since he didn't make the team.

Teeth and hair can also represent strength and power.

> *I'm not good at brushing my teeth. Sometimes I get scared that all my teeth will suddenly fall out. I have this dream that I go to school, and I smile,*

and I have perfect white shiny teeth. I close my
mouth, but when I open it again, people laugh
and point at me. I go to the mirror and I don't
have any teeth.

— Faye, age 9

A dream about losing your baby teeth may show that you are getting ready for a new stage in your development.

You may have heard the Biblical story of how Samson lost all his strength when Delilah cut off his hair. Many kids feel powerless and upset when their parents make decisions about their hair for them. Here's Lin's dream about a haircut:

They cut it so I look like a maniac. It's all weird.
When I look in the mirror, the mirror breaks!

— Lin, age 7

Hair is one of the most often mentioned points of conflict between young people and their parents. Dreams about hair and haircuts are very common.

When I was little my mom would brush my hair.
I'd have tangles in my hair and it would really
hurt. We'd yell and scream at each other, and I'd
feel really awful after. It was such a bad start to
the day. My hair means a lot to me. I judge other
people by their hair.

— Carla, age 10

If you dream about having your hair cut ask yourself:

◆ Have I felt weak or helpless recently?

✧ Have I lost something important to me?
✧ Am I worried about how others see me?

A dream about losing your wallet is similar. For most of us a wallet contains valuables, like money and ID cards. Ask yourself:

✧ Have I lost something that I value?
✧ Have I behaved in a way that isn't really me?
✧ Is someone trying to change me?

10. DREAMS OF EXPLOSIONS AND FIRES

There's a big thing, like an old furnace or something, in the hallway at school. There's something wrong with it and it isn't working. Someone throws a cigarette butt on the floor and the furnace starts to explode. I run home. It's going to explode all over the city. My family is running out of the house. We have to get out of the city. My dad runs back into the house. There's something he's forgotten.

— Keith, age 12

Explosion dreams suggest there are feelings "bottled up" inside the dreamer.

Keith was under a great deal of pressure from his parents, especially his father. Keith's father had been a top student and a star athlete, and he expected Keith to follow in his footsteps. The pressure to be like his father was building to a dangerous level in Keith. He had to find a safe way to release pressure, and his dream was helping him to do this.

Fire dreams are about "hot" feelings. A key factor in understanding a fire dream is determining the nature of the fire.

◇ Is the fire contained and under control (such as a hearth fire or campfire)?
◇ Or is it out of control, destructive?

My sister and I are in a huge castle. There are no windows on the ground floor. There are lots of other people. I feel like there's some terrible danger. I somehow manage to see out and see people pouring gasoline around the base of the castle. I get my sister and myself out just before they start the fire. A terrible fire starts and the others are all burned alive. A huge section of the city is burned too.

—Kim, age 14

Kim had this dream after her sister took Kim's silver bracelet without asking, then lost it. This dream shows the mixed feelings Kim has towards her sister. She's burning up with anger, but she also feels protective of her.

Anger is usually experienced as a hot, fiery feeling. Other emotions may feel this way to you, too.

◇ What feelings does the fire represent?
◇ What would be a safe way to express these feelings?

Other Popular Dream Themes

OBSTACLES

> *I had this dream a lot when I was little. There was a girl who lived across the street. I really liked her. I wanted to go and see her, but in the dream there was no air. I could never get across the street because all the air was gone. I tried to do different things, like hold my breath, or run really fast, but I could never make it.*
>
> — Paul, age 17

Obstacles in dreams can take the form of squeezing through tunnels, swimming across rivers, crossing bridges or climbing mountains. They are always tasks that seem incredibly difficult or impossible to do.

If you have this kind of dream you could ask:

- ✧ What difficulties or challenges am I facing?
- ✧ What will help me overcome these difficulties?

ROMANCE

Remember when the thought of kissing a boy or girl was totally gross? As you know, things change as you get older — you start to have more romantic dreams:

I dreamed I was grown up and the boy I like was grown up too and we were sitting on a balcony together. I felt so good.

— Naomi, age 9

Romantic dreams help prepare young people for future relationships. They help you experience what it will be like to fall in love with another person.

I'm on my bike and the girl I like is riding on the back. A big golden eagle swoops down and carries her off. My bike becomes magic and it flies up. I go after the eagle and I save the girl.

— Cameron, age 10

Sometimes you may be surprised by a dream about somebody you don't like. But the dream may be showing you that there is something very lovable about this person.

If you have romantic dreams you can ask yourself:

✧ What do I find lovable about this person?
✧ Do I let others see my own loving nature?

FAMOUS PEOPLE

I dreamed that me and my family went to a skating special, and Kurt Browning was skating, and I was his girlfriend.

— Cheryl, age 13

It's wonderful to dream about being friends with a famous rock star, movie star or leader of a country. Some people dream they are invited to tea at Buckingham Palace or the White House. You might have this kind of dream when you are not feeling too good about yourself. These dreams remind you that you're special.

I dreamed I met Julia Roberts. She was really nice. She got sick and I had to fill in for her. That made me feel good.

— Ruth, age 9

If you dream about famous people, you can ask yourself:

- ✦ Have I been feeling down on myself?
- ✦ Do I let myself be the best I can be?
- ✦ Is there something I have in common with this famous person?
- ✦ Is there something I can learn from him or her?

FOOD

The first question to ask yourself if you dream about food is, Am I eating properly? Dreams can give you practical advice about your health. A 12-year-old girl dreamed:

I'm at a banquet and there are all these delicious foods, like cakes and whipped cream. But all I take to eat are prunes! I don't like prunes, but in the dream they are delicious. I had this dream while I was taking medicine that made it hard for me to go to the bathroom. The prunes helped!

You might dream about food if you are feeling empty inside. Your first attachment to your mother is through food, so food often represents comfort, love and security.

On the other hand, you might be feeling a real fullness — a satisfaction with life.

If you frequently dream about eating lots of food, you could ask:

- ✧ Is there anything I "hunger" after in my life?
- ✧ Do I feel lonely, rejected or forgotten?
- ✧ Am I in a situation that feels "nourishing" to me?

A bad dream is having to eat food I don't like.
— Ilana, age 11

If you are eating food that tastes bad in a dream, you might be "taking in" something — like an idea or value — that you don't really like. This is what happened when some of 13-year-old Ken's friends started stealing:

I dreamed there was something I had to eat. It was really disgusting. I hated it, but I tried to force it down. But I couldn't do it.

Remember, it is how you feel about the food in the dream that determines if what you are taking in is good or bad for you. Ask yourself:

- ✧ Am I trying to "swallow" something in my life that I don't like?
- ✧ Am I going along with my friends, doing something I don't really want to do?

> *I dreamed I was driving a bus. There were a lot of
> people in it. I felt happy driving it.*
> — Niko, age 12

Let's look at the different modes of transportation and what they can mean in your dreams.

Public transportation vehicles, like buses, trains, planes and ships, move a lot of people, all at the same time and in the same direction. It can be very reassuring to know that you are "going with the flow." However, travelling these ways doesn't allow you any individual movement.

In a car you can go exactly where you want to go. When Al, 17, stopped going to temple with his family, he dreamed:

> *I'm driving my dad's car, but I'm going the
> wrong way down a one-way street.*

When Al thought about the dream, he realized that not going to temple was his way of expressing his independence from his family — but that it wasn't really the right decision for him. He decided to look for a better way to express his individuality.

Even very young children sometimes dream about driving a car.

> *A guy takes my mom and I get her car keys and
> drive her car. I can't see over the steering wheel
> very well and I can't reach the pedals, but
> somehow I save my mom.*
> — Pete, age 7

Whoever is in the driver's seat is always an important symbol. That person, or that part of your personality, is in charge at that moment.

Ask yourself:

- ✧ Who is in the driver's seat? What is this person like? Reckless? Responsible?
- ✧ Is there a back-seat driver? Is someone else really controlling things?
- ✧ What is the condition of the car? Is it old? New? Big? Small? Do the brakes and steering work? Is there enough fuel? Is the car going too fast?

With a bicycle, you move entirely under your own steam. It might take you longer to get somewhere than in a car, but you have much more control over where you are going and how you are going to get there. Skis, skates, Rollerblades and skateboards are other modes of transportation that use your own energy. They symbolize fun, exhilaration and speed.

If you dream about riding a bike, skiing or skating, ask yourself:

- ✧ Are things moving too slowly for me?
- ✧ Am I skimming the surface? Do I need to look deeper into something?

BEING LATE OR MISSING THINGS

I'm with my friends and they say, "So how did you do on the math test?" And I say, "What

*math test?" I feel, Oh no, I missed it! I didn't
know anything about it at all!*

— Nicole, age 10

These dreams usually come when you are anxious about failure, or missing something important. Fern, age 8, says:

*If I'm nervous about doing math, I'll have a
dream that I'm not able to do it. But that makes
me study more, and I usually do better.*

And Nick, age 10, has learned:

*Whenever I have exams or I'm worried about
something, I dream that I am late for hockey
practice.*

Some questions to ask:

❖ What is it I don't want to miss?
❖ What am I worried about?
❖ What can I do to prepare myself?

DREAMING YOU ARE OLDER OR YOUNGER

*It's the first day of school. I'm supposed to be a
big kid, but I stay a little kid.*

— Lech, age 10

If you dream you are younger than you really are, perhaps something happened recently to make you feel helpless, like a baby.

Think about when you really were that age — was there something important going on then

65

that relates to this dream? Maybe something similar is happening to you now.

You may feel like you are a little kid again if you are learning something new. Dirk, age 8, had this dream when he was learning to skate:

I dreamed I was a baby and I was just learning to walk.

Some questions you can ask yourself:

❖ Am I worried about a task I need to do?
❖ Am I afraid that people see me as a little kid?
❖ Have I behaved in an immature way?

Many young people dream about being older than they really are:

It's neat to think who you are when you grow up. In a good dream I like who I am. In a bad dream I don't like who I am.

— Caroline, age 8

Dreams about being older can make you feel confident. They help you to prepare for the future. Nasreen, age 13, who wants to be an actress when she grows up, dreamed:

I'm in Hollywood. I'm 21, I'm tall. I live in a mansion. There are TV cameras all around, and reporters want my autograph. I'm a famous actress.

Jody, age 8, dreamed:

I'm a teenager. I like who I am. I can travel on the subway by myself. I get to do whatever I want.

✧ What can you do now to help yourself become the person you dream about?

TEACHING DREAMS

You're innocent when you dream.
— Tom Waits

Have you ever dreamed you were doing something bad — like lying or stealing? When you woke up, weren't you glad it was only a dream? Mark, 14, dreamed:

I have a science project to do for school. I play hockey with my friends instead. I think I can do the project later. But then I am in school and I realize I don't have my project done. My friend Dan has a really good project. I wait till no one is looking and put my name on it.

Mark was very upset by this dream. He knows that cheating is wrong. He thought the dream was telling him he was really a cheater and a bad friend.

Everyone is tempted to do bad things at one time or other. You are not bad if you dream of doing bad things, or good if you dream about doing good things. It is what you do about your dreams that counts.

Dreams let you experience all of your feelings without hurting yourself or anyone else. The great relief we feel when we wake up from a dream like this teaches us a lesson, especially when we're tempted to do wrong.

And dreams can teach you very practical things. When 11-year-old Jacques was learning how to use a computer, he dreamed:

All night long I practiced all the steps I had learned in class. That's all I did! But I was much better the next day. It was just like I had been practising in real life!

Dreams can also teach you to see things from another point of view:

I dreamed I was a mutant and I could turn myself into anything. I turned my mom into me, and I turned myself into my mom, and I did what my mom does. I didn't like it. There is so much work she has to do.

— Darcy, age 8

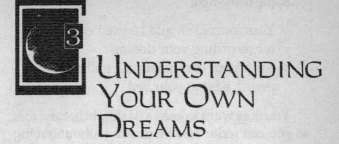

UNDERSTANDING
YOUR OWN
DREAMS

Now the fun begins! In this section you can learn the secrets to understanding what your dreams mean to you. You don't need any expensive equipment. There are no membership fees to pay, no application forms to fill out. But be prepared for some surprises. Dreams keep you on your toes. They can shake you up!

Before you begin, there are two things I suggest you do: start a personal dream journal and find a dream buddy.

YOUR PERSONAL DREAM
JOURNAL

The first step in learning what your dreams mean to you is to keep a record of them. Your journal can be a notebook, a loose-leaf binder or a box of index cards — whatever appeals to you. School notebooks or scribblers are a good size. Make it special by decorating it, or keep it plain and simple.

Some basic tips:

✧ Your journal should be used exclusively
   for recording your dreams.
✧ Keep your dream journal, and a pen or
   pencil, next to your bed.

You may want to keep a flashlight handy, too,
so you can write down a dream without having
to turn on a light. If you wake up and remember
a dream, write it down right away. Don't wait
till morning. There's a good chance you will
have forgotten it by then.

✧ Before you go to sleep, briefly note the
   highlights of the day in your journal.

Jot down what you did and felt — outline
is best. This background information will
usually help you understand the dream you
have that night.

Here's a sample from 14-year-old Eli's
journal:

— *school, have to choose courses for*
next year

— *lost science book*

— *swimming practice, worked on my*
turns

— *called J.* [a girl he likes]

— *mad at T.* [his brother]

✧ Always record the day's date. This will
  help you keep track of your dreams.
  Some dreams come in cycles —
  sometimes you will have the same kinds
  of dreams at certain times of the year.

Josh has upsetting dreams every year around
the middle of February. When Josh told his
parents about this, they recalled that there had
been a terrible fire in their house in the month of
February. Josh was 4 years old at the time, and
had been very frightened.

✧ Describe the dream in the present tense.

Instead of "I was lost in the woods and I was
really scared," write, "I'm lost in the woods and
I'm really scared." This will make the dream
seem more real to you.

✧ Write down as much of your dream as
  you can remember.

Don't leave anything out — no matter how
embarrassing it may be — and don't add details
that weren't really there.

✧ Give the dream a title.

After you have recorded your dream and
dated it, give it a name. Try thinking about the
dream as though it were a story or movie. What
title would best describe it? This will help you
discover the theme, or main idea, of the dream.

Find A Dream Buddy

A dream buddy is someone you can talk to about your dreams. It can be a friend or relative, but it must be someone you can trust. A dream buddy should never gossip to others about your dreams. Perhaps you and a friend would like to be dream buddies for each other. If you are a dream buddy, remember that it is not up to you to figure out the meaning of someone else's dream. Only the dreamer can do that.

HOW TO BE A GOOD DREAM BUDDY

- ✧ Listen carefully.
- ✧ Never make fun of the dreams you hear. Dreams are personal.
- ✧ Don't take anything for granted.

As you listen to your buddy's dream, try to imagine that you are from another planet and that you don't know anything about the people or things you are hearing about. You have to ask what everything means to the dreamer. If someone tells you a dream about a horse, your response should be, "What's a horse?" The more "silly" questions you ask, the more helpful you will be!

If there is no one who can be a dream buddy for you, use your imagination and create your own personal one. Sue, age 13, has an imaginary dream buddy who looks like ET! This is how she used her personal dream buddy to explore a dream:

SUE: *In my dream a witch comes into my room and steals my old teddy bear.*

DREAM BUDDY: *I'm from another planet. What's a witch?*

S: *A witch is an old lady who's really ugly and scary. She wears black and she does really mean things to people.*

DB: *What's a teddy bear?*

S: *A teddy bear is a toy bear that you have when you're little. It's soft and cuddly. When I was little I always slept with my teddy bear.*

DB: *What's stealing?*

S: *That's when you take something away from somebody, something that doesn't belong to you.*

DB: *Who feels like a witch to you right now?*

S: *My mom! She is being a real witch! All she does is criticize me. She's after me all the time. She's never nice to me anymore. She really does take away my good feelings!*

DREAM BUDDY QUESTIONS

At first, you may not be sure what questions a dream buddy should ask. So here are some suggestions to help you get started. You can make up additional questions as you go along.

✧ Who is in the dream? Are they people or animals? Describe them. Does anything in your life feel or seem the same way?

Kara, 14, dreamed about a bag lady, at a time when she was feeling as though no one liked her or wanted her around. Alice, age 13, had a dream about dolphins when she started her summer vacation. She felt free and playful, just like the dolphins in her dream.

✧ What objects are in the dream? Describe them. Does anything in your life feel the same way?

Dominic, 13, had a dream that he was trying to move a huge rock out of his way. Around this time, Dominic's parents refused to let him go to a concert with the rest of his friends.

✧ What activities are taking place? Describe them. Does anything in your life feel the same way?

Misha, age 11, dreamed about hamsters running on a wheel when he was feeling overwhelmed by his studies.

✧ What feelings do you have in the dream? Describe them. Do they surprise you? Why?

Harvey, 14, was surprised that he wasn't afraid when a robber came through the window in his dream. Sometimes it is the absence of feelings, or feelings that seem inappropriate, that point to the meaning of your dreams. For example, if you are in a dangerous situation but feel no fear, there might be some problem that you are ignoring. In Harvey's case, however, his absence of fear meant that he was becoming stronger and less fearful.

✧ Where does the dream take place? What are your thoughts and feelings about this place?

Louise, age 12, dreamed she was in a beautiful garden. She felt peaceful and happy and awed by the beauty in nature. She felt inspired to help protect the Earth.

✧ What action, if any, do you need to take?

Shelley, 14, had recurring dreams about her little sister dying or being kidnapped. Although Shelley loved her sister, she was resentful when her parents expected her to babysit for her sister on weekends. Shelley wanted to be with her friends.

When she realized that her dreams were expressing this resentment, Shelley decided to take action. She talked to her parents, who had not been aware of Shelley's feelings. They agreed to look for another babysitter.

Two Fantastic Dream Buddy Questions

These two questions can produce amazing results!

- ✧ Is there any wordplay in your dream?
- ✧ What associations can you make?

WORDPLAY

Wordplay is the creative use of words. Puns, for example, are a form of wordplay using words that have more than one meaning. Dream puns can be awesome — they're often incredibly clever and witty. They can really help you to understand your dream. Always be on the lookout for them!

Zoey, age 16, dreamed:

Me and my sister are in a store. I've got a charge card. (In real life I don't have one, but I do in the dream.) The salesclerk calls on the telephone to check it and says to me, "I'm sorry, but you're over your limit." Well, that just floored me, because I started this part-time job after school and on weekends, but it turned out they wanted me to work longer hours, and I just couldn't do it and keep up with my schoolwork. So when the salesclerk tells me I'm over my limit, that's really true! I can't keep working these long hours.

And 15-year-old Andy dreamed:

I wash my hair. While I'm drying it with my towel, I see some little brown things, like seeds in my hair. I look closely in the mirror, and I see they are little brown bugs, with shiny crusts on their backs, and they are moving. I think I have lice, I am freaking out, there are all these creepy insects on my head. I start to comb my hair and the bugs start to fall out. It is really gross! I call this dream "Bugs in my Head," and that's just how I'd been feeling the day before. I was working on this new computer program and I just couldn't get it! The computer kept crashing, it was really bugging me, and I remember thinking that maybe the program had a virus in it. So the computer was bugged, I was bugged and my dream was full of bugs!

Some other common examples of dream wordplay are:

- ✧ climbing the wall (frustration)
- ✧ sitting on the fence (indecision)
- ✧ chickens, or the color yellow (fear, cowardice)
- ✧ hot water (being in trouble)
- ✧ green faces or hair (green with envy)

ASSOCIATIONS

Another dream game you can play is called associations. This is easy to do, too. You just pick one of your dream images and let your mind play with it. Think of all the different things you associate with that image.

Eric, age 13, dreamed he was on board a spaceship:

> DREAM BUDDY: *What do you associate with a spaceship?*
>
> ERIC: *Okay, let's see. Spaceship: outer space, adventure, freedom, mystery, stars, Star Trek, new worlds . . . I guess that's about it.*
>
> DB: *Does anything in your life seem or feel like any of these things?*
>
> E: *I only wish! It's hard to have adventure and freedom when your parents worry about you all the time!*
>
> DB: *Can you think of anything that you can do that gives you some of the freedom and adventure you associate with a spaceship?*
>
> E: *When I ski, sometimes. And when I ride my bike. I think whenever I'm doing something intense, like sports, I feel that way.*
>
> DB: *Is there any action you can take?*
>
> E: *I could do more sports. I've kind of let them slip lately. I used to play more than I do now. I guess I miss it.*

Remember Jo Anne's dreams about cats in Chapter 2? Jo Anne associated cats with biting and scratching. When she thought about cats, she thought of her grandmother's house. She remembered feeling scared and lonely at her grandmother's house.

But Melissa's associations were completely different — cats made her think of warmth and softness.

Here's 12-year-old Lily's dream.

LILY: *I am with my friend Barb. We're in her room. It's really weird because her room is piled with stacks of papers, pens, pencils and jars and jars of glue. Huge, huge jars. In the dream I think, I never knew Barb had all this glue.*

DB: *When you think of Barb, what do you associate with her?*

L: *Barb's my best friend, she's smart and pretty and she's just really nice.*

DB: *What do you associate with the stacks of paper and piles of pens and pencils?*

L: *School, writing, essays. In real life Barb is helping me with an essay I have to do for school.*

DB: *And what do you associate with glue?*

L: *Sticking together! That's Barb and me!*

DB: *Anything else?*

L: *This is so amazing, because Barb is always telling me to "stick with it" when I feel like giving up on my essay!*

Did you notice that the jars of glue are a kind of wordplay?

Symbols stir up different associations in different people. By asking yourself what you associate with a dream image, you can discover more of what the dream means to you.

YOUR OUTSIDE LIFE AND YOUR INSIDE LIFE

Dreams can have more than one level of meaning. They can tell you about your outside life

79

and your inside life as well.

Sue's dream about the witch and teddy bear showed her her bad feelings towards her mother. This was the *outside* meaning of the dream. When Sue's dream buddy asked her some more questions, another level of meaning appeared to Sue:

DREAM BUDDY: *Do you ever feel like a witch?*
Ugly and mean?
SUE: *Well, I guess I do, sometimes.*
DB: *When was the last time you felt like a witch?*
S: *Well, probably when my mom gets on my case.*
I can act pretty witchy back.
DB: *Do you ever feel like a teddy bear? Soft and*
cuddly?
S: *Sure I do, lots of times!*
DB: *Well, how does the witch in you steal away*
the teddy bear in you?
S: *Oh, I get it! My witchy feelings take away my*
good feelings. So I'm doing to my mom the same
thing she's doing to me! I never saw that before!
Sometimes after my mom has yelled at me, she'll
say she's sorry — she wants to make up. But I
don't want to. I stay mad at her!

You won't always be able to find both levels of meaning in a dream. That's okay. The important thing is to ask the questions. If there is a deeper meaning to your dream, it will show itself eventually.

Some questions your dream buddy can ask you are:

- ✦ What's good in the dream? Can you find a similar good quality in yourself? How can you help that good quality get stronger?
- ✦ What's bad in the dream? Can you find a similar bad quality in yourself? What can you do to change it?
- ✦ Who would you like to tell this dream to? Why?
- ✦ Who would be the last person you would want to tell this dream to? Why?

RELAX AND HAVE FUN!

When you first begin to explore your dreams, you might feel a bit overwhelmed. There are so many questions your dream buddy can ask that at first you might think it's just a lot of work!

But dreams are fun to play with! They're like puzzles. You don't have to understand *all* the parts of your dream in order to understand its message. You just need to find one piece at a time. After a while you will have enough pieces of your own personal dream language to feel fluent. Then a whole new world will open up to you.

A DREAM JOURNAL CHECKLIST

To help you get started, I have created a checklist that you can follow for your first few times. Once you have gained confidence and are having fun, feel free to play with your dreams however you like.

A bit of advice: always open your notebook to a double page. That way you can write your dream on one side of the page and your notes about the dream on the opposite page. If you are using index cards, use two cards that you can place side-by-side. One card will be for the dream, the other for your notes.

Your journal might look something like this:

DAY'S EVENTS		ASSOCIATIONS
DREAM		OUTSIDE LIFE
TITLE		INSIDE LIFE
WORDPLAY		
		ACTION TO TAKE
FEELINGS		
		SYMBOLS

As you see, there are category headings on the pages. Each one represents a step for you to follow. If you divide all your pages into categories this way, you'll find it easier to organize all the pieces of information that you find.

Here's how 13-year-old Amy used the checklist:

DAY'S EVENTS

Before she went to sleep the night before, Amy wrote the date in her journal. She thought back over her day and jotted down in point form, "Handed in art project. Washed bike. Went to Dad's for dinner."

DREAM

Amy writes her dream down in the present tense: "I'm sleeping and I wake up because my mother is yelling at my brother to shut the door. I go downstairs. My brother Dan is making grilled cheese sandwiches. I look out the back door and see that the backyard is flooded. There is water coming in under the door."

TITLE

She thinks about the dream and decides to give it the title "The Flood."

WORDPLAY

Amy writes, "Cheesed off, big cheese." She feels "cheesed off" at her brother quite often, and finds he sometimes acts like a "big cheese."

FEELINGS

Amy leaves this space blank.

ASSOCIATIONS

Amy associates water with "bath, washing, sprinkler, hose." She remembers that she had been using the hose to clean off her bike the day before. Later, when she had come back home after having dinner with her father, Amy's mother had yelled at her for forgetting to turn the hose off.

OUTSIDE LIFE

Here Amy writes, "Forgot to turn the water off — could have been a flood."

INSIDE LIFE

Amy could just accept this dream at face value, but she takes it a step further. She imagines her dream buddy asking, "What is the dream showing you about your feelings?" Amy's parents are divorced, and Amy is still upset about this. In fact, she had cried herself to sleep that night after visiting her father. Amy feels that her brother gets to spend more time with her father than she does, and she often feels hurt and left out. Amy writes, "I have a flood of tears about Dad."

Then Amy goes back to the "Feelings" line. She writes, "Glad Dan's in trouble." In the dream, she felt happy that her mother yelled at her brother. But when she woke up, she felt guilty for feeling this way. That's why she'd left "Feelings" blank.

Although it's never pleasant to see things you don't like about yourself, it's better to face them than to hide from them. When you face things, then you can do something to change them.

ACTION TO TAKE

The dream has shown Amy that she needs to spend more time with her father. She writes in this space, "Tell Dad I want to visit more."

SYMBOLS

Here Amy writes "Water symbolizes feelings, tears." She will add this to her personal dream symbols list. I'll discuss keeping this kind of list later on in the chapter.

Amy will now be able to assert herself with her dad. In doing this, she will also become less envious and resentful of her brother. She will feel better about herself and have a better relationship with her father *and* her brother.

Here's another example, using 16-year-old Stuart's dream:

DAY'S EVENTS

Fight with Dad. He won't let me borrow the car.

DREAM

I'm in my dad's car. My dad's driving. It's raining and the traffic is really bad. There are all kinds of big trucks around. The car is going really slow, like we're hardly moving at all. Everybody is passing us. I look over and I see that the emergency brake is on.

TITLE

Going Nowhere.

WORDPLAY

Driving with the brakes on.

FEELINGS

Danger, frustration, stuck, going nowhere.

ASSOCIATIONS

Car: arguments. Lots of fights over the car. Dad won't let me borrow it.

Trucks: big, carry a lot of stuff.

Everybody passing us: that's how I feel about my life. It's passing me by. I can't live my own life.

OUTSIDE LIFE

My dad tells me I've got to be more responsible — I've got to learn to think for myself. But then he says, "Do what I tell you to do!" He won't let me drive the car, he won't let me live my own life.

INSIDE LIFE

Same as outside. Frustration!

ACTION TO TAKE

Negotiate with Dad.

SYMBOLS

Car = independence, freedom.

Stuart offered to wash the car every weekend in exchange for borrowing it. To Stuart's surprise, his father agreed!

As you practice with the checklist using your own dreams, don't worry if you can't answer all the questions. No one understands all of their dreams all of the time. If you find one or two pieces of meaning, that's great — you're on your way! But sometimes you might not find anything at all. That's okay. It happens to us all. Just try again with the next dream.

YOUR PERSONAL DREAM SYMBOLS LIST

As you fill in the pages of your dream journal, you will begin to see the connections between your waking life and your dream images.

Amy knows that, for her, water is a symbol for tears. Stuart links cars with freedom and independence. Jo Anne's list says cats mean something scary or hurtful, and Melissa's says cats represent warmth, softness and love.

Here is one of 12-year-old Marsha's dreams:

I go to get my hair cut. I only want a trim, but the stylist, who is someone I don't want to cut my hair, cuts it all off, so I have little tufts of hair sticking out all over, and it looks terrible.

Here's what Marsha has observed over time:

When I have this kind of dream it is a signal to me that I need to think some more about a decision I've made. It's like something inside me says, Wait a minute — you'd better think about this some more! In the dream I'm letting someone I don't like cut my hair, and I have this dream when I'm about to do something that I'll probably regret.

Marsha's dream glossary says, "Bad haircut equals bad decision." This doesn't mean that if you dream about a bad haircut that you have necessarily made a bad decision about something. But this is what it means to Marsha.

Sheri, age 11, has discovered that she dreams about people with missing or injured arms when she feels helpless. Nine-year-old Blair has found the same thing:

A monster is coming after me. It's like a dragon.
It has spikes and horns, ten claws on each foot,
red and yellow. It's trying to cut my arms off. I
have dreams like this when my parents argue. I
feel awful when they fight. I want them to stop,
but there's nothing I can do. I feel so helpless,
and I get scared they're going to get a divorce.

Blair also found a pun in his dream. The
monster was trying to "disarm" him — make
him harmless, helpless.

And Nadine, age 13, has observed:

When I dream that skinheads and punk rockers
are living in my basement, that's a sure sign to
me that I'm feeling really angry and rebellious. I
have to do something about it, or I'll get myself
into serious trouble!

Your personal dream symbols list will
quickly grow as you continue to explore your
dreams. But be sure to update your list
occasionally. Some of your personal symbols
may change over time as you yourself change.

HOW TO BETTER
REMEMBER YOUR DREAMS

Most people have difficulty remembering their
dreams now and again. It's usually just a temporary phase that passes with time. But if you are
having real trouble remembering your dreams,
these suggestions may help:

- ✧ Tell yourself several times during the day, Tonight I will remember my dream. When you are in bed, before you fall asleep, repeat it three times.
- ✧ On a piece of paper, write down a one-line wish for a dream. Put the paper under your pillow.
- ✧ Drink a big glass of water before you go to bed. This will make you wake you up in the night to go to the bathroom — improving your chances of catching a dream.
- ✧ Put a photograph or other small object under your pillow, and tell yourself you want to dream about it.
- ✧ When you wake up, don't sit up! Lie still and ask, What have I been dreaming? Moving around in bed when you first wake up interferes with dream recall.
- ✧ Record your dream on an audio cassette, if you have access to a tape recorder.
- ✧ Write down anything you can remember about your dream, even if it's a tiny scrap. Often, writing down just one word will bring more of the dream back.
- ✧ Be *interested* in dreams — other people's as well as your own. The more you pay attention to your dreams, the more dreams you'll remember.

✧ Ask your family members about their dreams. What does your mother dream about? Your father? Your brothers and sisters? Do you dream about the same things?

MORE DREAM PLAY

TELLING THE DREAM FROM A DIFFERENT POINT OF VIEW

This is easy and fun to do. The first step is to tell the dream exactly as you dreamed it. Then pick another point of view — someone or something from the dream — and tell it again from that perspective.

Does this sound confusing? It's not, really. It's exactly what you did when you were little and pretended that you were an animal or Iron Man or someone you saw on TV. It's what writers do when they tell a story with more than one character.

Let's use Sue's witch and teddy bear dream as an example.

DREAM BUDDY: *Okay, Sue, tell the dream exactly the way you dreamed it.*
SUE: *I'm in my bedroom. A witch comes in and steals my teddy bear.*
DB: *Now pick something or someone else in the dream.*
S: *Okay, I'll pick the witch.*
DB: *Now tell the dream again, but this time tell it*

from the witch's point of view.

S: I go into Sue's room and I see all her things
and I take her teddy bear.

DB: *Did anything change when you were the witch?*

S: Well, yes. I kind of liked being the witch.

DB: *What did you like?*

S: It felt good being so scary, like I had lots of
power. I felt strong.

DB: *Is there anything else in the dream you want
to be?*

S: This is neat! Yes, I'll be my teddy bear. Okay,
I'm Sue's teddy bear and I'm sitting on the shelf
and Sue is sitting on the bed and a witch comes
in and grabs me.

DB: *Did anything change when you were the
teddy bear?*

S: Yes, I was glad that the witch wanted me.

DB: *Why?*

S: Because Sue never pays any attention to me
anymore. She has so much stuff in her room. She
doesn't have time for most of it. She always
wants new things, but when she gets them she
just forgets about them!

DB: *Do you see anything differently now?*

S: That's incredible! I guess I could look after my
things better. I really do have a lot of good things.
And . . . my mom really isn't so bad. Most of the
time she's pretty good.

DB: *Is there anything you want to do, now, about
the things you have seen differently?*

S: I don't like to say this, but maybe I have been
pretty crabby and selfish lately. I could try to be
nicer to my mom. I know she cares about me.

You can try this with your own dream now.

Does anything change when you tell the dream from a different point of view? How does it change? You can tell a dream from any number of points of view. Each time you play a different part you will see the dream in a new way.

This exercise makes you use your imagination to discover other levels of meaning in your dream. When you tell a dream from a different perspective, you get to step out of your own shoes and see yourself in a different light.

HAVE A CONVERSATION WITH ONE OF THE DREAM CHARACTERS

Imagine that you are talking to someone, or something, in the dream. Remember, in dreams anything is possible. Animals can talk, people can fly, fish can walk. Dreams are like fairy tales or cartoons. Let your imagination work as freely when you're awake as it does when you're asleep!

Bob, age 15, had this dream:

I'm walking down the street. A man with dark hair passes by me. There is something funny-looking about him, about his eyes — they're round and bulging. They look a little bit like big fish eyes. I look back at him, and he turns around, and all of a sudden these long white strings like spaghetti come shooting out of his eyes and come right at me. In the dream, I know if one of the spaghetti things hits me, I will die. I run as fast as I can. Then I wake up.

Here is Bob's conversation with the man.

BOB: *Who are you?*
MAN: *Somebody you don't know.*
B: *What's the matter with your eyes? Why did
    you shoot that spaghetti stuff out of your eyes?*
M: *I have killer eyes. I can kill something just by
    looking at it.*
B: *Why do you want to kill me?*
M: *You know why.*
B: *No, I don't.*
M: *Don't be a jerk.*
B: *What do you mean?*
M: *C'mon, quit kidding. I saw what you did. I
    saw you cheat on your test.*

When he thought some more about the
dream, Bob also remembered the look on his
father's face whenever he did something wrong
— and how awful this made him feel. He also
associated this dream with the saying, "If looks
could kill . . ."

Here's 12-year-old Diane's dream:

*I'm carrying my baby brother. There is a big
black snake in the house. I run into my
bedroom and try to shut the door, but the snake
moves really fast and it gets in the room with
me and my baby brother . . . [This dream
made me] so scared I woke up. My heart was
pounding so hard I couldn't fall back to
sleep.*

Diane was surprised by what her snake had to say to her:

DIANE: *Why are you chasing me?*
SNAKE: *I have to chase you because you keep running away from me.*
D: *Why do you want to hurt me?*
S: *I don't want to hurt you. I just want to be with you. It makes me mad that you don't like me. I can help you.*
D: *How can you help me?*
S: *[Silence.]*

This was as far as Diane could get when she tried to talk to the snake. She knew that the snake didn't want to hurt her, but she didn't know how it could help her. So she couldn't imagine how the snake would answer her question.

If you reach a stalemate like this, you need to switch to another approach. Diane decided to take the snake's point of view. She tried to imagine what it would be like to be a snake.

DIANE: *I'm a big snake, people are scared of me. I can move fast. I'm down on the ground. People could step on me, but I move so fast they can't. I can see a lot down here. I can see what's going on. [Laughs.] I feel scary. I like being a snake.*

Diane felt good when she pretended she was the snake. She was surprised, because in real life Diane is afraid of snakes — she thinks they're slimy and repulsive.

Now, when Diane feels afraid, thinking of her snake friend makes her feel much better!

BECOMING A
MASTER
DREAMER

If you could have any dream in the whole world, what would it be? Would you choose to meet your favorite movie star or sports hero? Travel to another country — or another galaxy? How about a dream that would solve a problem or give you an idea for your school project? It's not impossible! Many people have learned how to master their dreaming minds, and so can you.

When you dream, you have access to everything you have ever heard, read, seen and experienced. Things that your waking mind has long forgotten and ideas that you have not yet put together are all available to you. And you can train your waking mind to tap directly into your "bigger" dream mind.

People from all walks of life have used the power of their dreaming minds for inspiration. Scientists, artists, writers, musicians and athletes have all learned how to use their dreams in this way.

Robert Louis Stevenson dreamed a story that

became *The Strange Case of Doctor Jekyll and Mr. Hyde*. A dream revealed the molecular structure of benzene to scientist Friedrich Kekulé — a discovery that began a revolution in modern chemistry! The musician Billy Joel has said, "I dream music. I don't always remember it but I dream it. The song 'The River of Dreams' — I dreamed it. I woke up singing it."

Mozart, Beethoven, Paul McCartney and Alexander the Great are only a few names from a long list of people who have been guided by their dreams.

Everything that you have ever experienced has travelled through your nervous system and been recorded in your brain. When you are awake, only a very small portion of this information is available to you — otherwise, you would be overwhelmed with thousands of thoughts, memories and ideas. But when you are dreaming, you have access to what is essentially a huge warehouse of knowledge.

Fourteen-year-old Edie's dreaming mind remembered where she had lost something:

This morning I awoke with almost no memory of my dream last night. I only remembered one small scene in which I find my long-lost gel pump in my exercise bag. Now, in real life, that gel had been lost for a couple of months — and the pump on it never worked. Also, yesterday I was thinking to myself that I had to buy gel, and wondering where I could have possibly lost it. Anyway, this morning I thought, Well, why not?

Let's see if my dream was right. Well, it was. My gel pump was right there in the exercise bag and I thought, The only thing that's off is that in my dream the pump works. So again I thought, Why not? And the pump worked without any maneuvering or anything. I couldn't believe it!

In becoming a master dreamer, you can learn to *control* the way your dreams turn out. It takes practice and commitment — many people give up after only a few nights. But it takes time to learn any new skill. Remember when you were learning to catch a ball? You probably dropped that ball hundreds of times before you were successful.

Most dreamers can bring about some kind of change in their dreams after just a few weeks, although results can be unpredictable at first.

I want to dream about horseback riding and I'll dream about riding a motorcycle. Or I'll dream about falling off a horse. Sometimes I try to plan the opposite. I tell myself I will fall off the horse so maybe I won't. This sometimes works, but usually it doesn't.

— Elizabeth, age 9

Although Elizabeth isn't successful every time, she is making progress. She's well on her way to becoming a master dreamer!

LEARN TO BE LUCID

A lucid dream is one during which you become aware that you are dreaming. This is a very special dream state. You can actually become the director of your own dream movie!

> *I'm in a maze. I know I'm dreaming. There are floating geometrical shapes all around me. Monsters — they look like demons — start chasing me. I tell myself to wake up, and I do.*
>
> — Anthony, age 12

If you have ever had a bad dream and told yourself to wake up, you have taken the first step towards having a full lucid dream. With practice, you can build on those few seconds of awareness and actually dream about anything you desire.

The first step towards lucid dreaming is learning to recognize when you are dreaming.

> *Sometimes when I've been having a really crazy dream I've asked myself, Is this really happening, or is this a dream? One time I said, This really is a dream! But then I got so excited I woke myself up!*
>
> — Dave, age 11

When you begin training yourself to have lucid dreams, it is important that you be relaxed. Your mind is more receptive this way. Just before you fall asleep is the best time to tell yourself, Tonight, while I am dreaming, I want to become aware that I am dreaming.

For your first lucid dream experience, give yourself a simple task to do in your dream, like snapping your fingers or turning on a light.

Remember, this is a dream. You can do anything you want!

> *I'm dreaming that I'm driving a tractor and all of a sudden I know I'm dreaming. And I think, Where am I going to find a light to turn on? So I give myself a flashlight!*
>
> — Jerry, age 14

When you have mastered these steps, you will be able to direct your own dreams in any way you wish.

> *I'm walking with the people from the cartoon "Strawberry Shortcake," and we're jumping on these stones, but then I decide I don't like jumping on the stones, I want to do something else. So then I start to glide about three feet off the ground, and then I fly up this mountain and into a cave. That part was good.*
>
> — Thomas, age 8

When people first hear about lucid dreaming, they sometimes wonder if it could be harmful or dangerous. Trying to have a lucid dream is not harmful in any way. If you are not ready for a lucid dream, your mind will simply reject the dream suggestions.

For example, in one of my early dream groups, a number of people wanted to experiment with their dreams. We decided that every night each of us would ask for a flying dream. The first night I dreamed that I just shot up into the air and came right back down to earth in about two seconds! In the dream I said, All right, I've got my assignment out of the way, now I can get on with what I really need to dream about!

Another member of the group dreamed that he went to the airport but he was told at the ticket counter that he couldn't fly because his luggage was too heavy! He understood this to mean that he had "baggage," or problems, to deal with before he could use his valuable dream time for flying.

CHANGE THE DREAM

I am sky-diving and I lose my parachute. Just before I hit the ground I remember I can fly!
— Rasheed, age 11

Try this if you have a bad dream. First, decide how you want to change the dream. What do you want to happen? For example, in my falling dream I decided that I would let myself fall. Rasheed chose to change his falling dream into a flying dream. He told himself that if he started to fall in a dream he would fly instead.

Carrie, age 10, had bad dreams that she was locked in a room and couldn't get out. She decided she would find the key. She dreamed:

I am in a room and there is no way to get out. I start to panic, and then I remember that I can find the key. I look at the door, and there's the key, right there in the lock!

Here's how Esther, age 8, changes her dreams:

A lot of times when I dream, it feels like I'm falling into something. It's all black and it feels really scary. So now, when this happens, I look for things I know, like my mom, or my couch, or my table. I think to myself, This isn't so bad, I know these things. It helps.

Once you have settled on how you want to change a recurring dream, tell yourself several times a day, Tonight, if I dream I'm lost, I will find my way, or, Tonight I will unlock the door. Then again, when you are in bed, repeat it three times.

If you don't succeed at first, don't give up! It takes time to control your fears. If you get discouraged and give up, nothing can happen. Be patient and keep trying.

FACE THE DREAM MONSTER

Another way to change a frightening dream is to tell yourself that you are going to face whatever it is that's frightening you.

Everyone has had dreams about being chased by a monster or someone scary. These are always awful dreams to have. Whenever possible when you have this kind of dream, *be active*. You will always feel better if you confront and conquer than if you run and hide. Tell yourself that the next time someone chases you in a dream, you will not run away. You will face the monster. If you can see what it is you are afraid of, you'll have a better chance of overcoming it.

Sometimes when we face our own monsters they change right away. Remember when Diane's snake turned out to be her friend?

Here are some other suggestions that can help:

- ✧ Give the monster a name. A nameless fear is worse than one that has a name.
- ✧ If you are too frightened to face the monster alone, bring some dream friends into the dream to help you. Think of someone who could help you face the monster. Tell yourself that the next time you dream of the monster, a dream friend will help you.

Sam dreamed:

I almost get killed by a giant man-eating hamster. My friend's dad saves me. He's from Japan. He uses swords. He cuts the monster up, and we eat him for dinner!

— Sam, age 7

- ✧ You can also dream up an object to protect yourself with.

I'm on this bus with my friend and my brother and my mom, and it tips over and falls into the water and we all go into the water, and I think, Uh-oh, water, could be sharks here. And then I see a fin come up and I hear the music from Jaws

*and then I have the idea that I can control the
dream. A shark comes, and it starts circling
around my mom, so I give myself a big laser gun
and I shoot at the shark and it vaporizes!*
— Daniel, age 15

⋄ Ask the monster to give you a present.
⋄ Make friends with the monster.

Simone, age 8, had terrible nightmares about
a grey wolf that chased her. She tried to
understand what the wolf might represent, but
nothing seemed to help. Then her dream buddy
suggested that the wolf might really be there to
protect her. Simone thought about this, and that
night she dreamed:

*The wolf isn't grey anymore. He's changed into a
white wolf with beautiful blue eyes. We play
together and he is nice.*

⋄ Ask yourself if the monster could
  represent something in your waking life.
⋄ Draw the monster.

Sonhi, 7, drew her dream monsters. There
were spiders, snakes, a giant and a kind of Darth
Vader creature. She drew them as they appeared
in her dreams — chasing and attacking her. Then
Sonhi drew more pictures, this time of herself
chasing and killing the monsters. She was
amazed and happy when her bad dreams
stopped soon afterwards.

Remember, if you feel helpless in a dream,

you may feel there is nothing you can do. You may not want to think about your problem. But the problem will still be there, whether you think about it or not! The only way to overcome your helpless feeling in a dream is by working out your problem. Once you confront and conquer fear in your dreams you can then transfer that successful experience to your everyday life!

> *I am in bed and I hear a creaking sound from the door, and then I see two long white fingers on the door, and I'm really scared, and then the door swings open and there are all these guys. They're all wrinkled and their skin is greyish white and they're in blue suits — like prisoners' suits with numbers on them — and they're in line, and they come marching in. And I jump out of bed and I kick the first guy in line and they all fall over. And then more of them start coming in through the windows and I fight them off. And then I woke up with a smile on my face. I felt triumphant, I felt so good!*
> — Rory, age 15

SOLVE THE PROBLEM OF RECURRING DREAMS

> *I was swarmed by a gang last year. They took my jacket and my shoes. I still have nightmares about it.*
> — Abdul, age 15

There are two kinds of recurring dreams. The first kind is caused by trauma — a severe shock or injury.

Soldiers often have recurring dreams about their terrible experiences at war. Natural disasters, car crashes, crime and physical and mental abuse are all traumatic events that affect people's dreams.

Sometimes the dream makes the dreamer relive the whole experience over and over again. This often happens when the dreamer has not yet recovered from the incident. (If you have been a victim of trauma and are experiencing bad recurring dreams, you may need help to work through your feelings. Speak to a counsellor.)

The second kind of recurring dream, and the more common type, deals with an issue that the dreamer has not yet resolved — a problem that needs to be overcome, or a need to look at something differently.

I have a recurring dream that I get chased by my shadow. I might be picking flowers and then I see a shadow. It's not of my body — it's hard to explain — but it's what I fear and stuff. It comes and then chases me and then it turns into someone who looks just like me. We play together but she never lets me touch her. If I touch her she turns into what I fear again. Like if we are playing ball and she has the ball, and then I go to get it from her. And if I touch her then the ball drops, and she turns back into the thing I fear. And then I keep running and running. For some reason I know not to play with her when she turns into the girl, but I'm pulled toward her because in a way she's me. She looks exactly like

*me in every way except for one thing. She's sour,
and in the dream I'm all sweet, and that's really
freaky, because they're both part of me. But it's
like we can't be one.*

— Toby, age 8

Like most of us, Toby sometimes has difficulty dealing with the "sour" side of herself, as her dream so beautifully illustrates.

There are many things you can do to resolve this kind of dream.

❖ Look in your dream journal to see when the dream occurs. Perhaps it happens before exams, or at holidays, or on your birthday. Or maybe it comes after you see someone you don't like, or do something you don't really want to do. Knowing this kind of background information will give you clues to help you solve the dream mystery.

Sheera, age 9, has this recurring dream:

*There is a war on. Sand is blowing all over the
place, like in the desert. It's awful, I'm all alone.
I've had this dream since I was about three years
old. When I wake up I go and sit on the stairs. I
don't know why, but this makes me feel better.
But I notice now that when I go to bed really late,
like eleven o'clock, I'll have this dream.*

❖ When you start to feel you are gaining some understanding of your dreams, go back to the beginning of your dream journal and see if the earlier dreams make any more sense to you. Usually you will be able to understand them a little more clearly at this point.

Using your current understanding of your dreams, look back and try to see which things were "disguised" and which you dreamed in a clear and straightforward way. This will help you to understand which ideas are difficult for you to accept and which you are more open to.

✧ Take note of any symbols appearing at predictable times. What do you dream about before exams? Before holidays? While you're sick?

When an idea "clicks," it is right for you. If it doesn't feel right, don't accept that meaning.

✧ Take action. Once you understand what the recurring dream is about, the next step is to do something about it.

MYSTERY DREAMS

It's possible that you can try all these suggestions and still not understand a dream. That's okay. Don't expect to understand all of your dreams all of the time. Nobody does. Of course, you might be surprised to discover the truth about a dream three or four months after it takes place. But some dreams will remain mysteries.

A dream that is mysterious will often feel very special. You'll just know it's important — even though you can't understand it.

It's in olden days. I'm wearing a pretty dress with a tight waist and a full skirt, a shawl with a little fringe, a bonnet and a parasol. My friend is in a blue dress like mine. It's me in the dream, but I look different. I'm older and I have blond hair. We walk along a dirt path and go into the forest. There are birds singing. It's more beautiful than anything you could see in real life. We come to a river. The water is really clear. There is something like a white stone in the water. It starts to move and I get scared. I start to run, but the white thing stings me in the palm of my hand. It hurt so much I woke up, and I could still feel the pain in my hand. I felt happy even though I got stung. The whole dream, I just felt so light. I know it meant something important, but I don't know what it was.

—Liza, age 11

These dreams are wonderful because they can remind you that life itself is full of mystery, surprise and unexpected possibilities. If you keep up your interest in dreams, one day the meaning of your mystery dream may be revealed to you.

Making Dreams Come True

Sometimes our dreams show us things that seem wonderful, but impossible ever to attain. Yet many people have made their dreams come true. They never lose sight of their dreams, and they never give up trying to make them real. Here are some tips to help you bring your dreams into your waking life:

- ❖ Paint or draw your dream images. Use clay or Plasticine to sculpt them.
- ❖ If you dream about someone you haven't seen or talked to in a long time, call or write a letter.
- ❖ Continue the dream in waking life. Think about ways you would like the dream to end. Is there anything in the dream you would like to change?
- ❖ Try to uncover the problems in your life that your dreams are expressing. Try to do something about them. For example, don't just accept it if the dream seems to be expressing how much you hate school. Take it further. What can you do to change how you feel about school? What help do you need? Who can you talk to about your difficulties?
- ❖ Keep the magic of your dream alive! Remember your dreams, think about them and take them seriously.

A FINAL SUCCESS STORY

When Albert Einstein was in his early teens he had an extraordinary dream.

Adolescence was a very difficult time for Albert. He did so poorly in school that he actually failed math! His parents were enormously unhappy with him. They wanted him to give up his academic studies and become a plumber, so he wouldn't be a financial burden to them. It was during this rough time in his life that young Albert had the following dream:

I was sledding with my friends at night. I started to slide down the hill, but my sled started going faster and faster. I was going so fast that I realized I was approaching the speed of light. I looked up at that point and I saw the stars. They were being refracted into colors I had never seen before. I was filled with a sense of awe. I understood in some way that I was looking at the most important meaning in my life.

It was this dream that would eventually inspire his theory of relativity!

Many years later, when asked about the important influences in his life, Albert Einstein related his dream and said:

I knew I had to understand that dream and you could say, and I would say, that my entire scientific career has been a meditation on my dream.

Isn't that something? A dream inspired one of the greatest scientific achievements of mankind.

Now, if you just take the time to look and to listen, imagine what marvels your dreams could bring to you!

ACKNOWLEDGEMENTS

I want to thank the many young people who have so generously shared their dreams with me. I especially thank Rachel James, Lorne Sussman, Sarah and Kestra Illiatovitch-Goldman, Layah and Sasha Singer-Wilson, Rowan and Corey McNamara, Brendan, Julia and Jennifer Smith, and Heather and Jamie Bond for their thoughtful contributions.

I also wish to acknowledge Marion Woodman, Dr. Ann Faraday and Dr. Patricia Garfield. The work of these three women has both influenced and inspired me.

I am grateful to Chérie Smith, who transcribed my notes and rescued me from countless computer disasters.

And finally, my deepest gratitude to my children, David and Lynette, and to my husband Thomas, for their unwavering encouragement, support and love.